101
Weird
Ways
to Make
Money

101 Weird Ways to Make Money

Cricket Farming, Repossessing Cars, *and* Other Jobs *with* BIG UPSIDE *and* NOT MUCH COMPETITION

STEVE GILLMAN

WILEY

John Wiley & Sons, Inc.

Published by John Wiley & Sons, Inc., Hoboken, New Jersey.
Published simultaneously in Canada.

Cover design: C. Wallace
Cover images courtesy iStockphoto and the artists: Golf Ball © Dan Thornberg, Classic Car
© Jane McIlroy, Beer Bottle © Uyen Le, Royal Flush © Pavlen, Grasshopper © Tomasz Zachariasz,
Detonator and Dynamite © DNY59/MB PHOTO, INC., Shovel © Pixhook, Headstone © Andrew
Parfenov, Mannequin © Milos Luzanin, Pomeranian Dogs © Morten Normann Almeland

For general information on our other products and services or for technical support, please contact
our Customer Care Department within the United States at (800) 762-2974, outside the United States
at (317) 572-3993 or fax (317) 572-4002.

Wiley also publishes its books in a variety of electronic formats. Some content that appears in print may
not be available in electronic books. For more information about Wiley products, visit our web site
at www.wiley.com.

Library of Congress Cataloging-in-Publication Data:
Gillman, Steve, 1964–
    101 weird ways to make money: cricket farming, repossessing cars, and other jobs with big upside and not
much competition/Steve Gillman.
        p. cm.
    Includes index.
    ISBN 978-1-118-01418-9 (paper)
    ISBN 978-1-118-08574-5 (ebk)
    ISBN 978-1-118-08572-1 (ebk)
    ISBN 978-1-118-08571-4 (ebk)
    1.   Creative ability in business.   2.   Success in business.   I.   Title.
    HD53.G49 2011
    331.702—dc22

                                                                                    2011002030

Printed in the United States of America

10 9 8 7 6 5 4

CONTENTS

Part Three
DIRTY AND UGLY JOBS

Part Six
HOME-BASED MONEY MAKERS

Part Seven
WORKING WITH PEOPLE

Part Ten
BUYING AND SELLING THINGS

Part Eleven
CLEANING JOBS AND BUSINESSES

Part Twelve
STILL MORE UNUSUAL WAYS TO MAKE MONEY

CONTENTS

Acknowledgments

I don't know what I would do without the loving support of Ana, the love of my life. Add to that the many hours she spent helping research the chapters here, and I owe her more thanks than I can offer on this page.

I also have to thank my editor, Richard Narramore, who pushed me to find real and accessible ways to make money that are still unusual or interesting so this would not be a book of untested ideas nor a routine employment guide. The book is better because of his suggestions.

Finally, thank you to all the individuals who participated in the interviews that appear in the book, as well as those who spent time helping me to understand the nature of the work involved in the jobs and businesses covered here.

INTRODUCTION

Some of the jobs, businesses, and investments covered here make millions for those who use them. Others are just profitable and interesting—better than another day flipping burgers or negotiating office politics. And who knows? Every billion-dollar industry had to have its first millionaire, so you too might be the first to really hit it big with a new and fun way to make money.

Who would have guessed, even a year before it happened, that we would see the first millionaire investor in virtual real estate? Ailin Graef used her avatar to buy and sell imaginary land for real money in the online fantasy game called *Second Life*. Players want better fantasy homes and are willing to pay real dollars for them. Real-world corporations rent billboards that occupy strategic locations in online virtual worlds. Ailin started with just $9.95—the monthly subscription fee—and built a virtual real estate empire worth a million dollars.

And who would think that frightening geese could be profitable? David Marcks had a job as a grounds superintendent for a golf course and had to get rid of hundreds of geese. He had the idea to use dogs, and after experimenting with various breeds, he found that border collies could be trained to do the job without losing interest (as the other dogs did). From that start, he developed and grew his company, Geese Police, to the point where it generated millions in annual revenue.

Some jobs and businesses covered here are not so weird. In those cases I try to find a different approach. Providing day care is not unusual, for example, but a real need exists in some areas for day-care services that specialize in caring for children with developmental disabilities. Or consider power-washing. It has become common, but it's possible to specialize in washing garbage trucks or travel trailers. "Normal" ways to make money suddenly have less competition—and more income potential—once you come at them from a new angle or find a new niche.

I have a good personal example of how a seemingly small niche can make money because of the lack of competition. Just prior to moving to Arizona, I bought lunch for my brother Chris and took notes as I questioned him about every aspect of carpet cleaning, a business he had been in for years. Once we settled in our new home in Tucson, I spent a few days putting together the web site www.HowToRemoveCarpetStains.com, which, as its name suggests, offers tips for removing stains from carpet.

From that point onward, I spent perhaps a few hours annually working on the site, eventually adding general carpet-care advice. Visitor traffic was slow to grow, but the site made about $30,000 profit in its first five years. I don't recall the last time I spent more than a few minutes working on it, but last month it made more than $1,500 (and it's just one of our many sites). Making web sites is old news, and everyone is doing it, but this shows the potential of a low-competition niche.

With that said, I have to also admit that not every niche—in jobs or businesses—is a good one. Some are likely to leave you struggling financially no matter how smart or motivated you are. Based on my experience, these tough niches include playing chess for money, picking fruit, and web sites about metaphors. That's okay though. I have enjoyed all three of these, and the pocket money they made for me was just a bonus (and my www.metaphorology.com makes enough money monthly to buy us dinner). It's great to build wealth, but you also have to enjoy what you do.

The moneymakers covered here have been carefully selected. Most are at least a bit weird or uncommon and therefore have less competition than most jobs or businesses. All of them are real ways that people have made money. I aimed for interesting, available in most areas, little money needed, little training needed, and potential for above-average income. Some entries meet *all* of these criteria, but all of the ways covered here meet at least several of them.

MONEY

You'll find a section with the above title in each chapter. The profit potential of some of the occupations covered here will be obvious, but some key ways to realize that potential will be pointed out. What about the less lucrative jobs and businesses? My advice is to use them for what they are: enjoyable ways to make some money, and steps toward bigger opportunities. For example, if you work as a bartender with the best shifts at the right clubs, you can have fun making a decent living, but if you want riches, you are free to use this as a means to someday own a chain of bars or nightclubs. And who knows where worm grunting, diaper cleaning, or mural painting might lead.

Work as an employee and then become the boss. This theme appears again and again in this book. High incomes are rarely found in employment alone unless you become a pro football player or a movie star. Of course, a job doesn't have to make you rich if you really enjoy the work and it pays the bills, but it is also true that almost any job can be a training ground for creating future wealth if you treat it that way. Millions of business owners are right now training their future competition—their employees. If you are hired to market green funerals and you pay attention, you can someday own profitable funeral homes. A part-time job tearing down buildings can give you the knowledge and contacts necessary to start your own demolition company.

Look at the small businesses covered here in the same way. A web site about carpet stains might just barely pay the bills, but you can expand that into an Internet empire consisting of 40 or more sites. Making a couple of hundred dollars weekly as a magician working birthday parties is not the end of the line if you use the experience to eventually create a television show or to write best-selling books on magic. A snow removal business won't make you very much as a one-man venture, but you can put your profits into more equipment and employees.

Think as an investor too. Buying and selling used stuffed animals might not make you rich by itself (then again, who knows?), but the profits can be parlayed into bigger investments. I used to invest money with friends who bought and sold old cars, splitting the profits with me. Making $500 at a time wasn't thrilling, but I did save that money and eventually invested it into real estate to make bigger profits.

Put all these ideas together, and you'll see that I'm suggesting you purposefully engineer upward progress in your financial life. Use jobs to gain the knowledge, the people access, and the skills you need for starting a business in a given field. Use small businesses to create larger ones. Use your investment returns to fund the next bigger investment. If you are seriously committed to doing so, you can make money with any of the ways covered here, and if it isn't enough by itself, you can use it as a step toward something better.

MY OWN STORY

Am I really qualified to write on different ways to make money? I'll tell you a few details of my life and let you decide.

At 6 years old I was an exterminator, killing flies in the house for a penny each at my mother's request. By 10 I was an arms dealer, collecting spent ammunition in the Great Paper Wad War and selling it back to the combatants—my brothers. By 12 I was running carnival games in the basement of my parents' house, charging money and offering prizes for ridiculously difficult games. Much of the paper route money earned by my brothers and their friends ended up in my first bank account. At 14 I became a loan shark, offering $2 loans to friends who had to repay me $3 in a week.

My penchant for finding ways to make money did not end in childhood. By 16 I was cutting and selling firewood with a friend, making perhaps $5 per hour, which seemed like a lot of money in 1980. At 17 I took my first real job as a short-order cook in a Big Boy restaurant and saved enough money to hitchhike to California and Mexico, among other destinations. By 20 I was done traveling for a while and took a job in a fast-food restaurant, quickly working my way into management after finding a better way to schedule, which cut $12,000 per year from the owner's labor costs.

About that time, I bought my first piece of real estate. I had a very basic idea that I had picked up somewhere. It was that you can buy for less when you pay cash and sell for more when you offer terms. A lot of people out there want to buy land or homes but don't have any money saved. This was before zero-down mortgage loans were being handed out by every bank and finance company.

I found a two-acre piece of land overlooking a small valley in some woods 30 minutes from where I lived. The real estate agent who owned it wanted $4,100 for it. I offered $3,300 cash, and we eventually agreed on $3,500. Closing a deal was much cheaper and simpler then, so a couple of days later the property was mine and I had perhaps $3,650 into it. I raked up the dead branches on the land and outlined a possible driveway in the grass using some logs. I took an old piece of plywood and painted on it: "For Sale: $4,750, $250 down, $100 per month, 11 percent interest," along with my phone number.

Two weeks later I sold it for exactly that price and those terms. I met the buyers in a restaurant to avoid closing costs. Selling the land for $1,100 more than my investment in just two weeks was fun, but I also collected that 11 percent interest for several years before the balance was paid off. Later in life I used the same strategy to sell a rental property for 15 percent more than I had paid for it just months earlier.

I had a variety of jobs around this time. I worked as a skip tracer for a collection agency, did some process-serving work (locating people being sued and handing them their summonses) for an insurance company, and became a blackjack dealer. I had "normal" jobs as well, like delivering pizza, landscaping, and driving a newspaper box route. But I always preferred the more unusual and interesting employment. Stealing cars in the middle of the night sounded both unusual and interesting, so I was happy to help out my brother when he started to do auto repossessions as part of his towing business.

At about midnight one evening, in my brother Jason's tow truck, we were cruising through a small town in northern Michigan. Behind a bar Jay spotted a Pontiac we were looking for. I jumped out with my flashlight and verified the VIN (vehicle identification number). Realizing that because the front wheels were turned the car was likely to hit the brick wall next to it if we tried to tow it, Jay decided it was better to enter the bar and ask the owner for the keys. I didn't like the idea, but he was probably right. I never felt comfortable with the ones we towed because they took longer, which meant the owner might do something—like the time a young man pulled a gun on us when were hooking up his Ford Mustang. When we had keys (from the lender), we could quietly sneak into a yard, and by the time the owner heard the engine start we were driving away.

The owner in this case was sitting at the bar staring into his beer as Jay explained that the bank would treat him better, and maybe even reinstate the loan, if he turned in the car voluntarily. No luck. In fact, no response at all. He just drank his beer. He wouldn't even turn his head in our direction. But his friends—who seemed to include everyone in the bar—were listening. A small crowd followed us back into the alley to watch Jay hook up the car and to yell a few insults at us.

Nervous because of the angry taunts, Jay pulled out quickly, and just as predicted, the front corner of the car caught the brick wall. A turn-light cover broke, and the crowd erupted, yelling and throwing things. I grabbed the baseball bat and ran through the drunks back into the bar, where I called the police. When I returned, Jay was on the roof of the tow truck, surrounded by the mob.

Fortunately, the police arrived quickly, but not quickly enough to prevent the theft of a toolbox from the back of the truck. They supervised as Jay dragged the car out, hooked up from the other end, and disconnected the drive shaft so as not to wreck the transmission when towing from the wrong end (the wheels were turned, making this necessary). Recalling that incident and others, it seems hard to believe what I would do for $15 back then.

Flash forward 15 years. After being a chauffeur, a real estate agent, and doing a 10-year stint as a part-time casino dealer (I've worked a full-time job for perhaps only 9 or 10 months of my life), I was taking some time off. I had cut down to one day of work each week, stuffing Sunday newspapers with ads for $100 every Saturday night. I had several rooms rented in my home, which no longer had a mortgage, and I had a few dollars in the bank, so it was time to travel again.

I went to Ecuador for four weeks and met the love of my life. A lot of paperwork and a few months later, Ana was here and my bachelor days were over at 37 years old. But the days of finding new ways to make money were not over. With renters depositing their money into our bank account, we embarked on several cross-country trips to find a new hometown and new ways to make a living. After a few normal jobs and residences in several states, we realized that we would be better off doing something more interesting and profitable, like starting a business.

Fortunately, like myself, Ana had had the entrepreneurial spirit since she was young. At eight years old she rented comic books to children who couldn't afford to buy them. With her grandmother she sold sandwiches to factory workers on their lunch breaks. They also sold homemade ice cream, popsicles, and Coca-Cola out of their house in Guayaquil, which was next to a school. Ana helped her grandmother sell "magic water," and in her teens she sold homework services and was a ghostwriter of love letters. When I met her, she was giving Spanish lessons to tourists while finishing college.

Early in our marriage, we brought back backpacks full of hand-carved Tagua figurines and fish-scale earrings from one of our trips to Ecuador. Tagua, also known as vegetable ivory, is a harder-than-wood nut from a palm tree, often carved into animal and other forms. Fish-scale earrings are made from, well, fish scales. They're dyed various colors and are actually quite attractive. We sold both at craft shows and flea markets.

We had a lot of fun working the flea-market circuit in Michigan. We sold dozens of different products. Ana made crafts to sell, and she discovered that we could triple our investment on Barbie dolls we found at rummage sales and thrift stores. I created Canned Critters, which were small stuffed animals trapped inside canning jars—kids insisted that their parents buy these so they could release the poor animal. I also sold hundreds of walking sticks that I carved and prepared from trees I cut. In the end, as much fun as it was, we discovered that the heyday of the flea market was long past (except in a few niches), and vendors who used to make $600 daily told us they hoped for $150 now, thanks to dollar stores and the Internet.

The Internet. That was where we needed to focus our efforts, we decided. There were some problems with this plan. To start with, I disliked computers and couldn't type. To this day I type with just two fingers. Also, we knew nothing about making a web site. What was HTML? How do you get people to your web sites, and then how do you make money? Still, we liked the idea of a portable business, especially since Ana hated the idea of another winter in Michigan.

We had invented a game called Deal a Poem, hoping to license it to a game maker, so www.dealapoem.com was the first domain name that we registered. The game never made a dime, but the web site we started to market it (and which made only a few dimes) helped get us into Internet publishing. Another early one of the 40 web sites we currently operate was www.HousesUnder FiftyThousand.com, inspired by our experiences traveling the country looking for a place to settle, and buying a beautiful home in a great little town in Montana for just $17,500 (which we sold six months later for $28,000). I started my web site www.IncreaseBrainpower.com around this time, too, which eventually generated an e-mail list of more than 32,000 subscribers to my *Brainpower Newsletter.* We used pay-per-click advertising programs to generate revenue. We soon moved to Arizona, and eventually to Colorado, with our new company: Webhiker LLC.

It was fun to write what we wanted and make money doing it! We were making only about $5 daily after six months, but then I discovered the power of distributing articles to promote our sites, and a few months later we were making a living. Currently some of our sites singlehandedly make more than any job I've had. I also started writing and selling e-books. Ana created TuSuperacionPersonal.com, a Spanish-language site with self-improvement articles. I created *Unusual Ways,* a newsletter for UnusualWaysToMake Money.com, to write about the many jobs and businesses that we and others have tried. That led to this book, and I hope you're holding onto the 30,000th copy sold, in which case I've found another good source of income.

By the way, just to complete my résumé, I should tell you that in addition to the ways mentioned thus far, I've made money as a property researcher, can collector, landlord, poker player, food vendor, postal worker, house renovator, contract laborer, road construction flagman, sample distributor, convention host, construction worker, restaurant equipment installer, factory worker, thrift store employee, carpet cleaner, drywall installer, apple harvester, adults-with-special-needs supervisor, banquet setup worker, product packager, mover, and more. Some of these jobs and ventures lasted just weeks, which was fine with me. On to the next one . . .

I love reading about all the ways people make money, and I especially like the less common occupations. But apart from being interesting to read about, unusual jobs and weird ways to invest or do business have some distinct advantages. To start with, it's more fun to make money doing some of the things in this book, versus sitting at a desk or on an assembly line five days every week. What about the dirty jobs that don't seem too fun? A common advantage with these is a lack of competition. You can get rich providing necessary services that nobody else wants to provide. And perhaps normal jobs aren't quite right for you. Many of the jobs and businesses in this book require a unique set of skills and interests. You might find something that you never considered but that makes you want to get up and go to work every morning. I did. I even gave up writing longhand and learned to like computers.

PART ONE

FUN WAYS TO MAKE MONEY

$\mathbf{Y}$ou can find fun in any work—although I don't recall finding any as a real estate agent. Of course, some ways of making money are more entertaining and exciting than others, and which ones they are depends on *who you are*. I enjoyed tracking people down when I was a process server, and I even made some money playing chess. Currently I have a lot of fun writing on my favorite subjects.

This section covers work ranging from bounty hunting to making a hatful of dollar bills as a street performer. The focus is on the fun, but many of the following activities hold real potential for making big money—if you approach them with the right attitude. Making beer for a brewpub is just a nice job, for example, but with experience and a few of your own recipes you can start a new brand. Some craft brewers have built multimillion-dollar companies from small starts. And tearing down or blowing up buildings might be a blast as a $12-per-hour job, but you can also use the experience to start your own successful demolition company.

NEVETTE MICHAEL, CRAPS DEALER

Nevette Michael works at Turtle Creek Casino in northern Michigan. I worked with her many years ago (at another casino), but even after weeks of training I couldn't handle craps, so I dealt blackjack and roulette. Nevette not only can handle her job but also clearly loves the work, as you'll see in this interview:

What did you do before casino work, and how did you become a craps dealer?

I was working full-time for a commercial photographer, running the office and occasionally helping where it was needed. My coworker . . . had been hired part-time at our little local casino and was loving the job . . . both the thrill of the game and the money. . . . He told me they were still hiring, so I interviewed for the dealer position (blackjack) and was immediately asked to training class. It took me another two years (and all the other games knowledge) before I tried craps training. . . . It took me six months before I could be on the floor for an hour without making a mistake!

Do you still enjoy the work?

After 19 years working in the casino, craps is still my favorite game. Nothing is more exciting in the whole place than a hot craps game executed by competent dealers who are smooth and having fun with the entire table. There are still many days I walk out to the table and my customers say, "There she is, my favorite dealer!" Not too many jobs where you feel the love like that!

How much do you make now, and what do starting dealers typically make?

I could be making twice as much if I chose to live in a bigger market. Still, I make enough to pay the mortgage, put food on the table, and take a few adventure vacations. . . . My base rate has been topped for the last nine years at approximately $10 per hour. We average $11 per hour in tips. . . . I believe they start at a base wage of $5.50 per hour plus tips ($16.50 per hour total).

As far as you know, do most casinos still do their own training of dealers?

Certainly here in my little neck of the woods. I've heard that there are actual schools in Vegas, but I believe those are only high-paid employment services in reality. Most casinos train their own and/or hire experienced dealers.

Is dealing blackjack or craps something anyone can learn to do?

If you've got basic math skills and are sociable, you can deal blackjack. Craps is another matter entirely. Not only do you have to have superior math skills, you have to be able to multitask, listen to many people tell you what they want you to do with their bets (sometimes all at once!), keep the game secure, and still be able to entertain. It takes a special personality and special skills to be able to deal craps.

Have you had opportunities for promotion to pit boss or other positions?

I have had the opportunity to "advance" to a management position, but it does not pay as well as dealing. Still, after dealing for so many years, I was interested in running a pit/sitting box for variety and, yes, more job security. As a dual-rater I mostly deal (and mostly deal craps), and on occasion I am a pit boss.

There are opportunities to deal casino games on cruises or in exotic locations. Have you considered working elsewhere, and have many of your coworkers done so?

When I first started . . . the casino business was just beginning to open up all over the country. . . . Many went to Chicago riverboats, Florida cruise ships, Vegas, Mississippi, and other Native American casinos. . . . Of course I've fantasized about making more money, seeing other places, but Traverse City is a wonderful place in so many ways for me . . . biking, kayaking, skiing . . . and is one of the best places to raise a boy. Maybe when he's off to college I'll reconsider my options. . . . Winters are awfully long!!

What advice do you have for a person who wants to be a casino dealer?

Feel comfortable with your math skills and just love to work with people. People come to the casino to be entertained, so give 'em a good time whether they win or lose. Toughen up your skin and let any negativity roll off your back. A warm smile works wonders!

CHAPTER 1

STEALING CARS FOR
FUN AND PROFIT

AUTO REPOSSESSION

"**I**t's just the repo man," he told his son.

"But, Daddy, why is he taking our car?" the little boy asked. His mother was digging out a mitten frozen to the floor of the trunk.

"Son, we didn't make the payments, and when you can't pay for it, you don't get to keep it," he explained, and then he handed me the keys. It was rare for an owner to handle a repossession that well, and even rarer to see it made into a teaching moment for his children. This was one of the first repossessions I did during my brief stint as a repo man more than 20 years ago.

Often, cars were not handed over voluntarily. I snuck into driveways, yards, and parking lots to take them with keys or by tow truck. I was chased and I had guns pulled on me—all part of the adventure. It had to be fun, since the boss paid me just $15 per car. The job pays better these days, but conflict is still common.

Money

Some companies pay their agents a percentage of the repossession fee or bonuses in addition to hourly wages, so if you become good at what you do you can boost your income. To make big money, though, you have to treat the job as insider training, with the goal of owning your own company. You can do repossessions as a sideline to a normal towing business or as your specialty. Additional sources of revenue come from related services. With a fenced area to store cars for clients, you can charge a daily fee. You can also auction cars for clients, taking a percentage of the sale or a flat fee.

Some sources peg the average annual income of repossession agents at about $15,000, although this may reflect the part-time nature of many positions. Tow truck drivers average $42,000 annually, and often do repossessions. *Owners* of repossession or towing companies can make much more, of course, with a handful in the United States currently topping $5 million in annual revenue.

How to Get Started

Many repossession businesses don't have web sites, so look in the yellow pages under "auto repossession." Call towing companies, too, because car repossessions are often a sideline to towing. Smaller companies may be open to your offer to help out for free on a job or two, to prove you can do the work. In fact, some outfits might require you to ride along on a few repossession jobs before you are put on payroll in any case, just to see if you really want the job and can handle it.

If you want to start part-time—whether as a way to decide if you like the work or to learn about the business before investing—a small company can be perfect. Some towing companies do just a few repossessions per week. And if you *are* interested in repossessions as a business, it is best to work as an employee for a few months.

Resources

- www.repoman.com: Phone numbers and links to many repossession companies—a good place to start a job search. Also has information for business owners.
- http://en.wikipedia.org/wiki/Repossession: Covers the basics of the business and the relevant laws; the latter varies from state to state.
- www.ftc.gov/bcp/edu/pubs/consumer/autos/aut14.shtm: More detail on the laws involved in repossession, although from a consumer perspective.
- www.campingcompanies.com: An example of a successful repossession company, and a good place to get a job (employees get full benefits).

CHAPTER 2

DRINKING ON THE JOB

SPECIALTY BEER BREWER

Yes, a brewer, sometimes known as a brewmaster, really does have to taste-test the beer he makes. If you like that idea, here is more good news: Beer-making jobs in small pubs and microbreweries have become available across the country in the past decade. In addition to drinking on the job, another benefit is the exercise. Unloading and carrying sacks of grain and hops will keep you in shape. The job also requires malting, milling, mashing, boiling, fermenting, conditioning, filtering, and packaging that beer.

Large breweries often require a degree in chemistry and hire only brewers with years of experience. Microbreweries are usually satisfied with certification from one of the good craft brewing schools, such as Siebel or the Institute for Brewing Studies. Some certification courses can be completed online in as little as three months—although you should look for one that also offers on-site training for a few weeks.

There are different ways to work in brewing. Some microbreweries now have hundreds of employees and positions for brewers and assistant brewers. It is probably easier to get hired at small brewpubs though. You can also work as a traveling brewer. Our local Irish pub recently lost its brewmaster, so it pays traveling expenses and $500 per batch for a brewer to come from California and spend a couple of weeks at a time working here in Colorado. He works at other pubs as well. We might call this position *on-call emergency brewmaster.*

Money

Although brewing beer has not yet made the list of professions tracked by the U.S. Bureau of Labor Statistics, the consensus in the forums at BeerAdvocate .com is that brewmasters are paid between $25,000 and $40,000 annually, and assistant brewmasters between $15,000 and $25,000. Filling in at small pubs and getting paid by the batch can provide a decent income along with travel opportunities.

Eventually owning a brewpub or starting a small microbrewery that distributes to bars and pubs is how you make bigger money with your skills. Of the brewpubs tracked by the business-data site Manta.com, more than 70 top $1 million in estimated annual sales.

How to Get Started

The University of Wisconsin and the University of California at Davis offer brewing courses. If you prefer a faster route to employment, try one of the online brewing courses, like that offered by the American Brewers Guild. For the cheapest and perhaps the fastest way into the industry, get a job at a brewpub and volunteer to help the brewer in any way you can. Offer to take on more and more responsibility. I know three people who brew beer in pubs, and two of them started in this way. It can also help to first experiment with brewing at home.

Resources

- *Homebrewing For Dummies*, Second edition, by Marty Nachel (Wiley Publishing, 2008): Start at home with this guide and see if you like brewing beer.
- http://en.wikipedia.org/wiki/Brewing: An explanation of the basics of brewing beer.
- www.siebelinstitute.com: Siebel Institute of Technology and World Brewing Academy offers online and on-site course in brewing.
- www.beer-brewing-advice.com: A large collection of articles on every aspect of beer brewing.
- www.pubcrawler.com: Catalogs breweries, brewpubs, and beer bars, along with reviews—a good place to start a job search.

CHAPTER 3

CREATING BEAUTY
AND THE BEAST

MAKEUP ARTIST

I was in Hollywood recently, being interviewed for a documentary about luck (I wrote a book on the subject), and I had to have makeup put on for the first time. The young woman whose job it was to make me look good came from New Zealand a few years earlier. She was doing contract work, meaning she was paid by the day for various projects. One advantage of making money in this way is that you have more freedom than as an employee. You can choose the projects you like, or to take time off when you like. A disadvantage is that your income is less consistent.

In addition to being a makeup artist for people appearing on television or film, there are many other niches you can work in. Makeup artists are hired to prepare brides and bridesmaids for weddings and to do high-fashion work for photo shoots. Then there are the classic special effects positions in Hollywood—making it look like an actor's arm has been blown off or his face burned, for example. This is perhaps the most creative niche you can get into.

Money

According to the Bureau of Labor Statistics, makeup artists average $45,010 annually, with 25 percent of them making more than $61,000. Fortunately the BLS provides additional information, so we know that positions at performing arts companies average $56,570, and makeup artists working for motion picture and video companies average $85,930—not bad pay for a fun job. Obviously, working in Hollywood is a worthy goal if you want to make more money at this.

As with almost any profession, you can make more money as a business owner than as an employee. Some self-employed makeup artists charge $400 to $600 per day, so even without employees you can make a decent living if you fill your schedule. Niches can be profitable too. You might specialize in working with politicians, for example. In October 2008 the *New York Times* reported that the makeup artist for vice presidential candidate Sarah Palin was paid $13,200 in the month of September 2008 alone.

How to Get Started

To get hired as a makeup artist, you'll generally need some sort of training and certification. Special effects makeup schools and colleges offer options from one-year certificates to four-year degrees. Targeted training classes around the Hollywood area can be as short as a month and typically cost less than $4,000, making this a fast-track way to get started.

Outside of the Los Angeles area, you can start by getting cosmetology training and then volunteering at local theaters. Having a year of real-life experience combined with a short-course certification can make you more employable than someone fresh out of a makeup college who has never worked in the field. You can also forgo the certification for special effects and just use your cosmetology training to start a business catering to brides and working in local television.

Resources

- *The Complete Make-Up Artist: Working in Film, Television, and Theatre,* Second edition, by Penny Delamar (Northwestern University Press, 2002).
- www.candacecorey.com: The web site and portfolio of makeup artist Candace Corey.
- www.makeup-artist-world.com: Offers home-study course. Also has articles on how to market yourself as a makeup artist and related topics.
- http://education-portal.com/special_effects_makeup_schools.html: Lists special effects makeup schools and colleges around the country.
- www.cinemamakeup.com: Offers hollywood makeup training of many types, including special effects courses.

CHAPTER 4

COUNT TO TWENTY-ONE

CASINO DEALER

I dealt blackjack, poker, and roulette for 10 years. Fortunately they let me work part-time, because I didn't care much for the job, even if it did pay off my first mortgage. On the other hand, I can tell you without a doubt that many of my coworkers loved the work, yet another example of how we are each unique and need to find the jobs and/or businesses that fit who we are.

Is casino dealing right for you? It might be, if you like people. Customers will sometimes be friendly, sometimes rude. They will sometimes share their good luck with you, and other times accuse you of plotting against them (really). You'll watch them win or lose thousands of dollars in minutes. You'll stand for long stretches (although hourly breaks are the norm), but at least the smoky environment I used to work in is becoming less common. If your hands work and you can count to 21, you can learn to deal blackjack. From there you might become a craps dealer, or move to the poker room, or even run a roulette wheel.

Money

The most common pay structure is a base hourly rate plus a rate based on all tips collected by all dealers divided by all labor hours for the week. In those cases the pay is the same regardless of which game or table you are assigned. But if you get hired by one of the rare casinos where you keep your own tips, you might get $5 in tips for the evening when operating the money wheel, or $500 in tips if you have a few lucky players on a $25-minimum blackjack table. In those cases try to get assigned to high-stakes tables and busy shifts.

Government statistics say gaming dealers average $20,290 annually, but they can't count unreported tips. Fifteen years ago, at the small tribal casino where I worked, even starting dealers made more than that. The statistics do show that 10 percent of dealers make more than $32,000 annually (I suspect this, too, is low), so aim to be in that 10 percent. Ask employees what they make, and if you have a choice, apply at casinos where dealers make the most money. Good dealers can eventually become gaming supervisors, who average $48,920 annually. While writing this I looked at many job listings, and one—on a cruise ship—guaranteed $165 per shift, which is about $43,000 annually if you work full-time.

How to Get Started

You can graduate from a dealer training school in a few weeks. The resources section that follows has an example of one. You can also find a casino that trains its own new hires, which is most common at smaller casinos, like those run by Native American tribes across the country. At the moment, most advertised positions require a high school diploma and a year of experience. Get that year in at a smaller casino and you'll have job opportunities around the world.

Resources

- *Dummy Up and Deal: Inside the Culture of Casino Dealing* by H. Lee Barnes (University of Nevada Press, 2005): A look at casino gambling from the dealer's side of the table.
- www.casinocareers.com: Job listings from casinos across the land (and sea).
- www.worldcasinojobs.com: Casino jobs around the world, and a directory of casinos around the United States and the world, so you can contact them directly.
- www.casinodealercollege.com: Dealer-training school in Arizona, Colorado, California, Michigan, and Singapore. It claims to place 100 percent of its graduates who are actively seeking gaming employment.

CHAPTER 5

MAGIC MONEY

PART-TIME MAGICIAN

On Friday nights at a popular pizza parlor in our town, a magician goes from table to table doing amazing tricks. Alas, this being a small town, I doubt he is paid much by the restaurant. He does make tips, though, and my guess is that the little bit he makes for his three hours is not the point. The point is that he likes his work and he is there to promote himself. When people ask him about performing at birthday or office parties, he naturally produces a business card.

If you like to be the center of attention, this can be a great way to make extra cash. Sure, most people won't make it big as a magician. But it's a fun, low-risk business you can start part-time, and for those who do more than dabble, the upside potential really is huge. You can educate yourself fairly cheaply, spend a little on supplies, practice, and get to work. Of course, you'll invest a lot of time if you want to be a good magician. But this can be at your own pace, and you can easily start this career without quitting your job, since most gigs are on weekends.

Money

Government data doesn't track the wages of magicians, since they're primarily self-employed, but some magicians' web sites advertise rates. They vary according to the type of magic done, the type of event they perform at, and the skill and experience of the magician. Some of the prices I found advertised are $140 for a 40-minute show, $125 per hour for a strolling magician (for large gatherings), and $125 for a two- to three-hour restaurant gig (visiting tables one by one). A typical charge for children's parties is $100, and these performances last 40 minutes or less. A street magician recently told me he made more than $2,000 in tips doing magic for 10 days during the annual Sturgis Motorcycle Rally in South Dakota.

If you do two restaurant gigs every weekend at $125 each, you'll make $13,000 in extra income annually. Get good at both the magic and the marketing of yourself, and this can become a full-time profession. Recently, in Las Vegas, we were in an audience of 300 people at a magic show that cost $24.95—one of the cheapest of many magic shows in town. Multiply that by 300 and then by 10 shows weekly, and that's more than $3 million annually for the casino. I suspect the magician was paid well.

How to Get Started

A lot of free information is available online, including videos demonstrating card tricks, levitation techniques, and much more. A book or two can speed up your progress, and you'll probably want to invest in props and manufactured magic tricks. Practice alone at first, and then test the patience of family and friends. The next step is to volunteer for a party or two and use these to develop and refine your performance. At the point when people start asking how much you charge, you're ready to start booking those gigs at restaurants, birthday parties, and corporate get-togethers.

Resources

- *Magic For Dummies* by David Pogue (Hungry Minds, Inc., 1998).
- www.magician.org: The International Brotherhood of Magicians; tons of information here.
- www.mrmagician.co.uk: You can start learning magic tricks here.
- http://zachwaldman.com: Zach Waldman had paid gigs as a restaurant magician by age 14.
- www.the-restaurant-magician.com: An online course, not on magic tricks, but on how to make money as a magician.

CHAPTER 6

EXPLODING ON THE JOB

DEMOLITION WORKER

I once had a job tearing down an old house with low-tech tools. A section of pipe worked for ramming out walls, until the roof was standing on just a skeleton of two-by-fours. I pushed on it gently and watched as the house crashed to the ground. Of course, there was still a lot of hard work at that point, but I was surprised at how much fun it can be to demolish things.

That was a small demolition project, and my partner and I did it with nothing but a pickup truck, a crowbar, hand tools, and that piece of pipe. According to a recent article in *Entrepreneur* magazine, the start-up costs for a small-scale demolition service run $2,000 to $10,000. That covers workers' compensation insurance for employees, general liability insurance, and some basic tools—and probably assumes that you already own a pickup truck for hauling scrap to the dump. Sheds, barns, and other buildings can be demolished without heavy equipment.

Large-scale demolition involves tasks like using explosives to carefully drop a whole office building to the ground without hurting surrounding structures. This work can also include bridge demolition, asbestos removal and disposal, and the dismantling of all sorts of dangerous structures. As a business owner, you need years of experience and a lot of money to invest in heavy equipment. But you can start as an employee.

Money

In Labor Department statistics, demolition workers are lumped together with construction workers. As a category, the average annual wage is $33,190. Wages vary significantly by region, though, from a low of $24,000 in New Mexico to more than $49,000 in Alaska and Hawaii and more than $54,000 in the New York City area.

Naturally, the bigger profits are in starting your own demolition business. Some companies start with small demolition combined with junk-hauling and construction cleanup services. Multimillion-dollar businesses in this field have had small starts, as you can see from the examples in the resources section.

How to Get Started

To get hired by a demolition company, you might first need some experience in related areas. One of the easiest to get into is construction cleanup. It's the least-skilled, lowest-paid position in construction companies. You'll sort and dispose of scrap materials and sweep up at building sites. When I was younger, I found these jobs through a temporary agency because the construction companies sometimes don't want to hire employees who are needed only for a week or two at the end of a project.

If your aim is to start a demolition business, take notes as you work. You'll have to learn about regulations and permits and other legal matters as you work in the industry, since these change over time and by location.

Resources

- *Demolition: Practices, Technology, and Management* by Richard J. Diven and Mark Shaurette (Purdue University Press, 2010).
- www.ehow.com/how_2078412_start-demolition-business.html: How to start a demolition company, and links to other relevant articles.
- www.controlled-demolition.com: An example of what's possible. Controlled Demolition Inc. took down the Kingdome in Seattle, the largest building ever demolished by implosion.
- www.interiordemolition.net: Interior Demolition Inc. started small with interior-only demolition (knocking out walls for room expansions, etc.) and grew into a full-service demolition company.

CHAPTER 7

MAYBE IT'S NOT SO FUNNY

RODEO CLOWN

You have to really like excitement to be a rodeo clown, and it doesn't hurt to have quick reflexes as well. Imagine trying to purposely make yourself the target of an angry 2,000-pound bull in order to protect a rider who has just been shaken off that animal. That was the job description, by the way.

As a rodeo clown—sometimes known as a rodeo protection athlete—you'll wear protective gear under bright and loose-fitting clothes that are designed to tear away. The clown makeup, and some of the clownish behavior, is for entertaining the crowd, not the bull. You will often work with one or two others. One of you will be the barrel man, meaning you will get the bull to chase you and then jump into a padded barrel that you hope will protect you. In case you're considering what country to work in, keep in mind that they do not generally use protective barrels in Australia. It's sometimes possible to work primarily as a comedy clown, entertaining the crowd while the other rodeo clowns do the dirty and dangerous work.

Money

Wages vary widely, and rodeo clowns are typically self-employed. It is common to make about $100 to $250 per show, depending on experience and the venue. It is also common to pay for your own travel expenses. A 2008 article on MySanAntonio.com, about the wages of local sports figures, reported that rodeo clown Luke "Leon" Coffee made $75,000 annually on the national circuit.

You can supplement the usual performance income in several ways. For example, "Backflip" Johnny Dudley works as a paid spokesman for rodeos, doing many radio and television interviews and other public appearances. He also puts company logos on his clothing for a fee and offers advertising space on his 44-foot clown trailer, which he refers to as a "rolling billboard." Of course, if you become somewhat famous you can parlay that into bigger fame. Louis Lindley was well known as a rodeo clown for 20 years, which led to a movie career under the stage name Slim Pickens. You might have seen him in the cult classic *Dr. Strangelove* or in *Blazing Saddles*.

How to Get Started

Before you seriously consider this as a career, you should be sure you know what you're getting into. Watch some videos of rodeo clowns in action (see the resources section) and attend a few rodeos. Jobs in this field are rarely advertised, so talk to rodeo clowns to see who is hiring and what their requirements are. While you're at it, ask workers in the industry about their medical costs and where they buy health insurance. Finally, get in shape for this job before you start. You want to be able to move fast and not tire easily when a ton of wild animal is coming at you.

Resources

- http://en.wikipedia.org/wiki/Rodeo_clown: A brief explanation of the history of rodeo clowns and the nature of the work.
- www.timbertuckness.com: Timber Tuckness has been a rodeo clown for decades. Check out his videos here.
- www.backflipjohnny.com: "Backflip" Johnny Dudley calls himself "one of the most marketable and professional rodeo clowns in the industry."
- www.prorodeo.com: The Professional Rodeo Cowboys Association; information on events and videos.

CHAPTER 8

THE BUSINESS OF
CHASING CRIMINALS

BOUNTY-HUNTER

I was a skip tracer many years ago. Sometimes confused with bounty hunting, skip tracing is simply finding people. I did this primarily by phone when working for a collection agency, and I had to actually physically locate the person being sued when I was a process server. Bounty hunters, also called *bail-enforcement agents*, use skip-tracing techniques, but their job is more interesting and dangerous than simply locating someone.

They are primarily hired by bail-bond agencies. Suppose a court sets bail at $50,000 for someone charged with theft. A bail-bond agency might charge the accused $5,000 (and sometimes require collateral), and then give or guarantee the court the $50,000, which is forfeited if the defendant doesn't make it to trial on time. In this case, rather than lose the $50,000, the bondsman pays a bounty hunter 10 to 15 percent of that amount to find the defendant and bring him to jail to await his next court date. This can be difficult and dangerous work, but bounty hunters catch as many as 31,000 bail jumpers per year, with an almost 90 percent success rate.

Money

The question of how much you can make is a difficult one. It obviously varies with your success rate and how many cases you handle. If you work for a bounty hunter as hired help, you might be paid by the job or get a percentage of what he makes. Several web sites estimate annual income at between $50,000 and $80,000 for bail-bond agents, but without reliable sources. Suffice it to say that some full-time bounty hunters pay all their bills with their work.

Bigger money is made with running your own bounty-hunting business, and is also a function of the size of the bail in each case. A job that pays

10 percent of a $200,000 bail bond can make for a good month. Of course those larger fees usually come with more dangerous bail jumpers. Finally, other revenue sources include starting your own bail bond agency, writing about your work, or getting famous. Dog the Bounty Hunter, of the television show by that name, certainly makes more from his program than he ever did as a bail-enforcement agent.

How to Get Started

You need a license in some states, while others don't require any formal training or licensing; only a contract with a bail bondsman is needed to start working. California requires a background check and training courses, and bounty hunting is illegal in Kentucky. Ask a local bail bondsman what the laws are in your state and what you can do to train for and get hired to do this work. These jobs are not typically advertised.

Clerical work in either a bounty hunter's or bail agency's office is a good way to get a feel for the industry and for that particular employer. It is best to start with a team or at least one other bounty hunter, rather than trying this on your own.

Resources

- *Modern Bounty Hunting: A Real-Life Guide for the Bail Fugitive Recovery Agent* by Rex Venator (Paladin Press, 2005): A book by a guy in the business.
- www.bountyhunt.com/new_hunter.htm: A guide to getting started put together by a professional bounty hunter.
- http://en.wikipedia.org/wiki/Bounty_hunter: A decent overview of the history of bounty hunting and relevant laws, plus a lot of links to more information.

CHAPTER 9

HILARIOUS INCOME

NICHE COMEDIAN

If you made all the other kids in school laugh—and that was your intention—you just might be a comedian. Perhaps it is time to hone those skills and start making some money. In addition to comedy clubs, comedians are regularly paid to perform at private parties, corporate events, bachelor parties, fund-raisers, birthday parties, colleges, seminars, wedding receptions, and in cruise ship lounges.

As a comedian you get to express yourself in creative ways. You might choose to create comedy with a political message, or make music or magic tricks part of your show. You can specialize in performing for certain groups or in certain settings. The talent agency ComedianBookings.com lists the following categories and more: corporate comedians, comedy troupes, comedians for universities, clean comedians, comedy acts, female comedians, hypnotists, jugglers, political humorists, Jewish comedians, and ventriloquists.

As you can see, you can find your niche not only in the type of comedy that you do but in the places you perform. You might, for example, become known for your outrageously raunchy routine and specialize in working adults-only resorts and cruises. You could also do just kids parties, with a clean routine that involves puppets or some other gimmick. You might be the first comedian to make it big without ever appearing in public, promoting yourself with online videos and selling CDs and video downloads from a web site.

Money

Comedians often start with comedy club gigs that pay no more than $50 or $100 for a 20-minute routine. If you're still at that level after a few years, it might be time to try something else. Fortunately, good comedians who know how to market themselves can make decent money. Funnyguyproductions.com, a web site where you can book a comedian for a party or other event, says there are fewer conservative or "clean" acts, so these comics can charge more. Its typical clean comedian gets $1,200 to $2,500 per show. ComedianBookings.com says its acts start at about $5,000 plus expenses, and some of its comedians get up to $100,000 per show. Your goal, then, if you want big money, is to get good, get famous, and hire a great talent agent.

How to Get Started

Study comedy, both with books and by watching it while taking notes. Few comedians can make a living with just a collection of random jokes. You should explore possible themes for your act, and find a niche that works for you. Practice your routine in front of a mirror and then in front of friends and family. Keep refining your act, and then look for open-mic nights at local coffeehouses, clubs, or bars. Be sure you get video of yourself performing. From there—and with video in hand—you can approach owners of comedy clubs to get gigs as the warm-up act. You may have to do this without pay at first, just to get exposure and see how audiences respond. Talk to other comics to learn about other potential venues. Talk to the most successful ones you can find to learn how they market themselves.

Resources

- *Comic Insights: The Art of Stand-up Comedy* by Franklyn Ajaye (Silman-James Press, 2002).
- www.standupbootcamp.com: Train with top comedians in Las Vegas.
- http://beacomediantips.com: Tips on becoming a comedian, preparing your résumé, and honing your skills.
- www.youtube.com: Search "comedian" and you'll find hundreds of videos.
- www.joshsneed.com: The web site of stand-up comedian Josh Sneed.

CHAPTER 10

JUGGLING BURNING
BOWLING PINS

STREET PERFORMER

One summer day, my wife and I watched a street performer in downtown Boulder, Colorado. He juggled various items, including burning bowling pins, while riding a six-foot-tall unicycle and joking with the audience. To a 10-year-old boy who volunteered to help with a trick, he said, "Now when you grow up you can do this, too—and live in a van just like me." We tossed a couple of dollars in his hat and asked him a few questions. He did several shows daily, and I saw him make about $50 to $60 from this one.

You don't necessarily need to learn magic or juggling to be a busker (another name for a street performer). You can sing, play guitar, do tarot-card readings, tap dance, break-dance, recite poetry, swallow swords, draw caricatures, and more. In Bisbee, Arizona, we met a man who had trained a mouse to relax on the back of a cat that was curled up on the back of a dog. For a buck or two he would let you photograph yourself with the whole peaceful animal pyramid.

One great benefit of being a street performer is the opportunity to see other places. Some street musicians travel the world, paying their way with the money thrown into their hats or guitar cases. Traveling to cities during festivals or other events can be very profitable because of the crowds.

Money

The income of street performers varies greatly. As I mentioned in Chapter 5, a street performer once told me he made more than $2,000 in 10 busy days doing magic tricks. Jesse Gersenson, a guitar busker who has played through-out Europe and the United States, says he makes $30 to $60 nightly in New Orleans for "three hours of lazy playing" and more during Mardi Gras.

He also says that a harmonica player he knows makes $100 to $300 daily. Some street performers claim good results from less competitive locations, like outside of churches after weddings, at flea markets, or at the entrance to supermarkets.

How to Get Started

If you can do something that people would like to see, get out there and start performing. Pick a few places where you would like to perform and check them out, talking to other buskers if possible. Street performers are welcomed in some cities, discouraged in others, and regulated in many. For example, to play bagpipes in the streets of Santa Monica, California, you need an inexpensive permit. Check with the local city hall to see what regulations exist.

By far, the easiest way to get started if you don't have a worthy talent is to create or buy an outrageous costume and collect tips from people who want to have their photo taken with you. We once paid a giant robot in San Francisco $2 so I could take a photo of my wife with him, and as we left Japanese tourists were taking out their wallets as well.

Resources

- *Juggling for the Complete Klutz*, 30th anniversary edition, by John Cassidy (Klutz, 2007).
- *Magic For Dummies* by David Pogue (Hungry Minds, Inc., 1998): Contains a lot of magic that can be performed on the street.
- www.buskerworld.com: A guide to busking, etiquette, tips, and more. Check out the history page and the list of famous buskers, too.
- www.buskersadvocates.org: A street performer advocacy web site, with legal information, news, and more.
- http://undercoverny.com: Stories and videos of street performers in New York.

CHAPTER 11

DIGGING UP OLD COINS

METAL DETECTING

Recently my wife and I visited a nearby duck pond that had been drained. The ducks and geese waddling nearby complained loudly, but the man working the dried bottom of the pond with a metal detector was happy. He said it had been 80 years since the pond was built, and this was the first time it was without water. His detector beeped repeatedly, and he kept pulling coins out of the ground. During those 80 years, visitors lost rings and other jewelry as they fed the ducks, and coins were thrown in for good luck. In the course of our five-minute conversation, the man dug up another six or seven coins to add to his bulging pockets.

Treasure hunters call it "coin shooting" when they use a metal detector to find coins, but old coins are just one of the treasures you can find. Valuable historical artifacts are regularly found. If you haven't tried metal detecting, you're missing out on exercise, adventure, and possibly an extra source of income.

Money

Popular beaches can have a fresh supply of treasure every day in summer. During the Cherry Festival in Traverse City, Michigan, for example, the beaches are packed, and I have watched as numerous treasure hunters gathered every night with metal detectors in hand. A friend tells me that she and her husband have found many gold rings, as well as the usual coins.

Metal detecting is most often a hobby, and my perusing of metal detecting forums suggests that if you can make $200 per month coin shooting on weekends you're doing better than average. But it can also be a way into other ventures. Historical research led treasure hunter Mel Fisher to the Atocha, a shipwreck with $45 million in coins and gold—but only after a 16-year search. More plausible ways to make money include writing books or creating relevant web sites. My own treasure-hunting site, listed in the resources section, is not a big success yet, but it makes more money than my coin shooting. Many successful companies also sell equipment and supplies. You can start such a business part-time and as small as you like, perhaps buying and reselling one metal detector on eBay, and building from that.

How to Get Started

A basic metal detector can be bought for as little as $100 if you buy it used, or as much as $1,000 if you want to start with a decent new model. As the story at the start of this chapter suggests, drained and lowered bodies of water are an insider's secret to profitable treasure hunting. Other places to try are parks, beaches, abandoned homes, and old schoolyards. You can learn more secrets by hanging out in treasure hunting discussion forums online.

Resources

- *The Urban Treasure Hunter: A Practical Handbook for Beginners,* Second edition, by Michael Chaplan (Square One Publishers, 2004).
- http://gometaldetecting.com: Tips and photos of old coins so you can see what you might find—or what you found but didn't recognize.
- www.coloradotreasurehunting.com: My own site, which goes beyond metal detecting into some of the more obscure types of treasure hunting.
- www.kellycodetectors.com: Detectors and accessories, including used and refurbished machines starting at less than $100.
- www.americandetectorist.com: Great information and a discussion forum.

PART TWO

MAKING MONEY OUTDOORS

When I was 17 years old and living in a cabin in northern Michigan, I heard about a company that paid $40 per ton for balsam fir tree boughs, which it made into Christmas wreaths. Thousands of acres of national forest surrounded me, and it didn't harm the trees to take a few of the lower branches from each, so I talked a friend into helping me with my new money-making scheme and we started cutting off branches. Five hundred pounds of fir boughs later, we realized it wasn't worth the effort.

Fortunately, you can find better jobs if you like working in fresh air and sunshine, or in rain and snow and cold. I managed to make $13 per hour picking apples at a time when the minimum wage was about a third of that (get paid by the box and work fast), and I did okay landscaping homes for a real estate investor. At the moment, I could sit out on the deck with the laptop to write this—but that might be pushing the definition of outdoor work. In any case, the jobs and businesses in this section will either keep you in shape, be low risk, have big profit potential, be fun, or all of the above, and all are done primarily outside.

DAVID MARCKS, GEESE POLICE

David Marcks is the president and founder of Geese Police Inc. In 1986 he and his brother Richard started experimenting with dogs to get rid of the geese that plague many golf courses, parks, and open grassy areas. That eventually led to the formation of David's company in 1996, which became Geese Police Inc. in 1997. Now owned by GPI LLC, the company has 35 specially trained dogs. It services New Jersey and parts of New York State, and there are also Geese Police franchises throughout the country.

I understand that your first dealings with geese were when you worked as a grounds superintendent for a golf course, and you eventually found that border collies could be trained to chase off the birds. How long was it before you turned that experience into a business?

Within a few months, I started doing it part-time and within a year I was working at it full-time.

How much training does it take to prepare a dog for this work?

A lot!! An untrained border collie would kill a goose as quick as look at it. Training takes about 12 to 16 months after they are a year old and have been socialized.

Does your company sell trained dogs or training services?

Only to our franchise owners/offices.

Do you offer other services and products besides dealing with goose problems?

No.

You and your franchisees must have a good chunk of the business where you operate, but is there much competition in others areas yet?

Yes, there are tons of copycats just in New Jersey. Hundreds of copycats elsewhere, but they come and go. We are the first company to use border collies in Canada goose control, and we are the largest and the best by far. Competition keeps you honest. It is not really competition because you can't compare apples to oranges. Others use all types of dogs and/or their pets and don't have the control that we have with our dogs. The competition thinks this business is just letting a dog out to "chase" geese by letting them out of the back of a truck. Our dogs herd the geese; they do not chase them. We know it is a whole lot more. We have fun with competition.

What are some of the advantages of buying a franchise from your company, versus a person trying to go it alone starting out?

Shortcut to a proven successful business. You have guidance throughout. You have to follow certain rules and regulations and state laws. You always have a reference, someone to call when you run into a situation that you do not have the answer for. Someone to lean on and give you reassurance. We assist them with finding these very valuable dogs. The industry is always changing, and we keep up to date with the changes.

What other advice can you offer a person who might like to get into this business either as an employee or an owner?

Remember, we make it look easy and that is called experience. There is so much involved in this business; it is not just the dog's training and maintaining the training levels. Keeping up on the federal, state, and local regulations. Again, it is not just getting a dog and a truck to do this job.

CHAPTER 12

HAVE FUN FRIGHTENING GEESE

GOLF COURSE BIRD REMOVER

In one day, a Canada goose can eat up to three pounds of grass, damage five square feet of turf, and leave behind a pound of feces that may carry E. coli bacteria. They love to congregate in parks, on lawns, on school playgrounds, and especially at golf courses. But as much as they might like to, golf course owners do not get to kill the geese and other birds that plague their greens. They have to find nonlethal ways to get rid of them. Several methods exist, but perhaps the most effective is to use trained collies. In fact, these dogs are so good at chasing away the birds without touching them, that even animal rights groups endorse this method.

This potentially very profitable business allows you to work outdoors and with animals. In addition to chasing geese, you will consult with owners of large open spaces about prevention plans. Geese congregate where they have food sources, so you'll post signs for clients, advising people not to feed the geese. Ultrasonic devices are available that deter geese from gathering, and you can lease or sell these to clients. Some companies also supply mute swans, which aggressively chase away geese, especially when they are nesting.

Money

Most companies determine the price for their service based on factors like the size of the property, number of ponds, and concentration of geese, so pricing is variable. Since geese typically return within weeks or months, long-term contracts are common. For example, a St. Louis company advertises several goose-hazing plans. One, meant for a property or subdivision with more than 100 geese and multiple ponds, costs $695 for the first month and $495 thereafter. That includes five visits per week the first month at random times, and three or more visits weekly after that. It offers an on-call service for those who don't want a contract.

You can also get into the industry in other ways. For example, you can sell repellent and other products directly to the public. You can sell ultrasonic goose-deterrent devices, fencing, and other supplies to goose control companies. You can make big money training and supplying border collies (the best breed for this work) as well, since they sell for $3,000 to $7,000 each. But even as a simple goose control service, you can make real money. In the Chicago area, Knox Swan and Dog LLC advertises that it has more than 300 properties "under the watchful eye of our Mute Swans and Border Collies," and New Jersey-based Geese Police Inc. has reported annual sales of millions of dollars.

How to Get Started

To get into this line of work as an employee, search "goose control company" online and you'll find plenty of examples, although you'll have to make a lot of phone calls to find those that are hiring (many are small family-run businesses). Even if you want to start a business in this field, the training and experience you'll get as an employee will make later success more likely. Geese Police Inc. (see the resources section) offers franchises if you want support and a proven system. The dogs may be the biggest investment you'll have, typically costing thousands of dollars each.

Resources

- www.geesepoliceinc.com: An example of a successful goose control company, and it offers franchises.
- www.birdbgone.com: Products for ridding an area of geese and other birds.
- www.wildgoosechasers.com: A goose control company that services clients in Illinois and Indiana.

CHAPTER 13

KILLING SMALL TREES

CHRISTMAS TREE SELLER

On the first spring visit to their cabin one year, my parents found that someone had cut and stolen a beautiful fir tree in the front yard, almost certainly during December. Yes, Christmas trees have become so valuable that you have to guard your yard when the season nears. Although the average price nationwide is about $42, a decent tree can sell for more than $100 in major cities, and more than 30 million Christmas trees are sold annually in the United States.

Starting a tree farm is one way to take part in this billion-dollar industry, but you will have 21,000 growers to compete with. Retailing the trees takes much less of an investment in time and money. Rent a small lot (ice cream shops that close for winter go cheap), buy a truckload of trees, and you're in business. If your spouse or children volunteer, you don't even need to complicate things with employees.

Several niches exist with less competition. You can sell trees for delivery online. Companies currently doing this ship by UPS or FedEx ground. You can rent out live Christmas trees to those who don't want to kill a tree. You can play middleman, paying the lowest wholesale prices possible and selling to small Christmas tree vendors who can't afford the large orders needed to get the best price.

Money

Online vendors get $75 to $150 for trees shipped directly to consumers. Live trees rent for $30 to $125 (plus a deposit) depending on type and size. With a rental business, you collect hundreds of dollars in fees before a tree grows too large to use—and then you can sell it for planting in someone's yard. Prices at traditional tree lots vary by region, from $30 to as high as $200 for premium trees. Your cost is important, of course. Firs and pines wholesale for $10 to

$18 at five to six feet tall, with discounts for volume. Shipping can add a dollar or more per tree, depending on distance and size of order. Watch for specials. As I write this, a grower in Oregon who needs to raise cash fast is offering 700 seven-foot fir trees for $8.50 each on an online bulletin board.

Experienced retailers suggest that 400 trees is a good first-year goal, with double that the second year if it goes well. If you pay an average of $15 per tree, and have rental, advertising, and other costs of $2,500 for the season, you'll invest $8,500 for a 400-tree lot. Sell them all at the national average of $42, and your net profit the first year will be more than $8,000 for about six weeks of work, and more than double that the second year if you sell 800 trees.

How to Get Started

Some tree farms offer to guide you through the process, rather than just sell you the trees and wish you luck. They can tell you what sizes and types are most in demand, how many typically sell in given locations, and what has worked for other retailers. Look for one of these helpful farms to start with, even if you have to pay a bit more for the trees.

Resources

- www.christmastrees-or.com: Industry information, including how to run a Christmas tree lot.
- http://livingchristmas.com: A company providing Christmas tree rentals.
- www.sandhillchristmastrees.com: A Christmas tree farm that offers free consulting for retailer clients.
- www.christmastree.org: National Christmas Tree Association; full of information and links to more resources.

CHAPTER 14

SWIMMING AT THE GOLF COURSE

GOLF BALL RECOVERER

At about 11 years old, my brother and a friend used to jump into the mucky ponds on a local golf course and gather golf balls. After washing them with soap and water, they took them back to the pro shop at the same course and sold them for as much as 50 cents, depending on the brand. Once they had made the huge amount of $20 or so, they moved on to other ventures.

Today, used golf ball retrieval is better than ever as a way to make money. Two types of workers populate the field. The first are the "poachers," who sneak into courses at night and scour the ponds and the surrounding terrain for balls. The professionals get permission from the golf course, sometimes paying the course owner 8 to 10 cents for each ball retrieved. Some people use rakes and other retrieval tools, but the ones who make the big money are usually using scuba gear. In southern areas this means risking alligators and venomous water snakes. Golf balls are collected by the hundreds and even thousands in this way. They are then washed in soapy water, sorted, and sold.

Money

Balls are sold according to condition and brand. To get top dollar, you have to sell them yourself, using Craigslist.com or eBay.com. They sell for as little as 12 cents each in poor condition, bought to be blasted into a lake one last time or for practice. Better ones sell for 25 cents to a dollar. For example, those advertised on Craigslist as of this writing are between 50 cents and a dollar in bags of two dozen or more. With the bid at $36.95 and a few days to go, there is this auction on eBay as of this writing: 36 Titleist 2007–2008 Pro V1x AAAA Used Golf Balls.

Your other option is to sell by the thousands. Big wholesale buyers have minimums. One current buyer, for example, asks for at least 15,000 gold balls in each batch you send. Buyers pay from 7 to 18 cents per ball, so you may have to collect from free sources, but good retrievers can collect several thousand balls daily, and who has time to sort and sell that many in the usual 36-packs sold on eBay?

How much potential is there? An article on scubadiving.com reports that golf ball divers make up to $100,000 per year. The article profiles Brett Parker, who dives for five hours daily and collects 3,000 balls at a time. One part-timer who doesn't dive reports on his web site that he made $100 to $125 every time he spent a few hours at the golf course.

How to Get Started

It is easiest to start without diving, naturally. You can check Amazon.com or eBay.com for a Golf Fisherman Golf Ball Retriever. You can usually find one for about $25. This device is thrown into pond or lake and pulled out with a rope, collecting balls as it slides across the bottom. More expensive retrieval devices are available that may work better. A scuba certification gets you into the big money potential when you are ready for that step.

Resources

- www.aaausedgolfballs.com: A seller of used golf balls, and it will buy them from you!
- www.underwatergolfball.com: Underwater Golf Ball Recovery Inc. will pay you weekly for the golf balls you collect.
- http://dayjobnuker.com/2007/09/05/how-to-making-money-selling-used-golf-balls: A fun story about making money salvaging used golf balls, with links to more information.

CHAPTER 15

MEDICATING MAPLE TREES

TREE SURGEON

A local tree surgeon was at the house across the street from us the other day, trimming a few branches. Two months ago he spent half of a day there, working with the various trees on the property, checking for disease, filling holes, and removing dead branches. A tree surgeon, also known as an arborist, and sometimes more colloquially as a tree doctor, is a tree specialist. Tree surgery is the treatment of diseased or damaged trees, often by filling cavities and/or pruning and bracing branches. If you like to work outside and want a better title than tree trimmer, this might be a job for you.

The tools of the trade include pruning shears, loping shears, pruning saws, pole saws, chain saws, sprayers, and ladders. The two biggest investments for most tree surgeons are a commercial-grade wood shredder and a truck. Whether you are considering this as a job or as a business, you should be in good shape and comfortable operating a chain saw while off the ground in a rope harness or on a ladder.

Money

Tree surgeons are classified with tree trimmers for statistical purposes, and the average annual wage for the group is $32,090. However, the top 10 percent of workers in this field make more than $47,650 annually, and tree surgeons are more likely to be in that group. Naturally, with your own business comes more potential income.

Tree removal can be a major profit center, with charges as high as $2,000 to remove trees in areas like Los Angeles. The average across the United States is less than $1,000. Other services offered by tree surgeons include fertilization and soil management, bracing, deer management, insect and disease management, shaping, lightning protection, stump grinding, and tree planting. Often arborists or tree surgeons specialize in certain services. In some areas, arborists charge up to $125 per hour for consultations. At least one tree doctor I discovered when doing this research makes money by speaking, training others, and doing seminars.

How to Get Started

College courses in forestry, agriculture, and arboriculture can help, but there are no formal requirements to become a tree surgeon. Without a degree or formal training, the most accessible position is that of tree trimmer. It's not a highly paid job, but it's a good way to learn what you need to start your own business. Of course, you should also study the written and online literature, and you might practice your new craft on the trees and bushes in your own yard.

Joining the International Society of Arboriculture can connect you with others in the business. And although becoming a CA (certified arborist) through the ISA is not a requirement, it can be a good move for marketing purposes. In addition to a written exam, it requires three years of documented experience, so start keeping records the moment you begin working in the industry.

Resources

- *The Tree Doctor: A Guide to Tree Care and Maintenance* by Daniel Prendergast and Erin Prendergast (Firefly Books, 2003): A good educational and reference text.
- www.artistic-arborist.com: A company that's "a full service tree and plant health management firm."
- www.arbordoctor.net: An example of a tree doctor in Minnesota.
- www.isa-arbor.com: International Society of Arboriculture, where you can get various certifications.

CHAPTER 16

CHOP WOOD, MAKE MONEY

SPECIALTY FIREWOOD SELLER

My friend had the truck and chain saw. I had a splitting maul and the energy of an 18-year-old (my age at the time). We got a free permit to cut dead and down trees on national forest land. We cut, split, and delivered seasoned maple firewood for $75 per full cord, dividing the profit equally after my friend was paid for the use of his truck and saw. That's how I covered my expenses when I lived in the woods of the Upper Peninsula of Michigan. Today, you should get a lot more than $75 for seasoned maple, and there are even better ways to sell firewood than by the cord.

The markup is much higher for small batches of wood and for special types. Firewood is sold in bundles of a few pieces, for campers. Some woods are used especially for certain types of smoking. These include apple, hickory, mesquite, and cherry. Alder is bought in large quantities by salmon-smoking businesses in the northwest. Whole white birch logs are bought for decorative purposes. In our part of Colorado, people buy pinyon pine for the wonderful piney odor it emits when it burns. If you specialize in one of these niches, you're more likely to get a price that makes it worth your time.

Money

When I cut firewood, two of us cut, split, and loaded a full cord (four by four by eight feet) in about four hours. Prices vary around the country and by type, and delivery may or may not be an extra charge. Some recent examples: Albuquerque, New Mexico: mixed white oak and cedar for $305 per cord. Riverside, California: a half-cord of oak hauled by the customer for $100. New York City: $100 for a fourth-cord of mixed hardwoods.

As suggested, you'll make more in the specialty niches and with small batches. Bundles of 10 small decorative white birch logs are sold for $25 in

East Coast cities. Smoking woods are sold in small batches too. Slab wood (the round parts cut off logs when making boards) can be bought cheap from lumber mills. A load that costs $100 can be cut to short lengths and packaged into about 200 small bundles using plastic. These retail for about $6 at gas stations in vacation areas and at campgrounds. You typically wholesale them for $4. That's $800 gross on each $100 load you break down and sell. Do a couple of loads (400 bundles) weekly, and you should clear $1,000 after expenses.

How to Get Started

You can cut dead wood for free on some public lands, although the Bureau of Land Management charges $10 per cord in some areas. Otherwise, you'll need to get permission to cut on private land (perhaps for a fee or in exchange for ridding the land of dead wood). A decent chain saw can be had for $200, and log splitters—much better than my splitting maul—start at about $250. A pickup truck is needed, and it can help to have a small trailer you can pull behind it as well. Read up on the various woods and how long they need to be seasoned (dried) before selling if you're not cutting dead and dry wood. Learn the terminology. A *face cord* is only a partial cord, for example. To prevent the spread of dangerous pests, conservationists recommend selling firewood within 50 miles of where it is cut.

Resources

- *The Backyard Lumberjack* by Frank Philbrick and Stephen Philbrick (Storey Publishing, LLC, 2006).
- www.legitimate-home-business.com/firewood-business.html: Information on starting a firewood business.
- www.logsplitter.com: Log splitters, chain saws, and other supplies for firewood businesses.
- www.nycfirewood.com: A company that sells firewood in New York City.

CHAPTER 17

WINTERTIME PROFITS

ROOFTOP SNOW REMOVER

Snow, when settled and compacted, can be as much as half water, and a cubic foot of water weighs 62 pounds. Thus, two feet of icy snow on a roof of 2,000 square feet can weigh 124,000 pounds—the equivalent of parking 30 cars up there. In researching this chapter, I looked at some nasty photos of roof collapses from snow—in Flagstaff, Arizona! People need that snow removed in many parts of the country.

This is a good business for those who need to make money in winter. If you landscape for a living, for example, this can keep income coming in from November through March. Some snowplowing or roofing companies do rooftop snow removal as one of their services, while others offer it as a stand-alone business. It requires relatively simple tools. A ladder, a long-handled snow rake, a plastic snow shovel, and an ice chipper are often enough. On a typical job, you remove most snow, clear vents as necessary, chip channels in ice dams to prevent meltwater from backing up under shingles, and sometimes spread nitrogen fertilizer above roof dams to melt some of the ice. You'll also clear away any snow that fell onto sidewalks and driveways during the process.

Money

The price for clearing an average-size roof of snow is typically $100 to $300. Ice-melting substances are separate charges. Billing by the hour is common, with some companies charging up to $80 per man-hour. At a more likely $60 per man-hour, on a roof that takes two workers two hours to clear, along with $10 in ice-melting materials, the total charge would be $250. I have personally cleared a roof of two feet of snow in less than three hours (when I was younger), suggesting that if you work fast and run a one-man show, you might do better charging by the job. If you can get $200 for a job in your area, for example, and spend eight hours doing three jobs per day, you'll make $600 per day, or $75 per hour. The work is very weather dependent and seasonal, but the pay can be good while it lasts.

A niche you might try is snow removal from the tops of semi-truck trailers. Special rakes are available for this job, so you never go up on the roof. Truck drivers are doing this largely on their own at the moment, to cut weight and increase gas mileage. If you get 20 jobs at a truck stop, you might be able to do this efficiently at a price that's affordable for the drivers and profitable for you.

How to Get Started

You can get into this business for as little as $200 for the basic tools. Liability insurance is a good idea, however, since chipping away ice dams has been known to wreck roofs if done incorrectly. In fact, with that risk in mind, it might make sense to work for a snow removal company for a few weeks to learn how to do it right. Offer to work cheaply just to get the experience.

Resources

- www.sima.org: Snow & Ice Management Association, a business association that provides information and certifications.
- www.servicemagic.com/task.Snow-Removal.40421.html: A snow removal service directory where you can list your business.
- www.avalanche-snow.com: Snow rakes and other tools.
- www.hollandroofingco.com/snow_removal.html: This Alaskan company gets $350 minimum for a rooftop snow removal job.

CHAPTER 18

PAID TO EXERCISE

BICYCLE-TAXI DRIVER

If you want to work outdoors, get exercise, and you like being around people, running a bicycle taxi might be right for you. Also called pedicabs or bicycle rickshaws, a typical bicycle taxi holds up to three customers, who are often tourists looking for a ride around the city or a park, or a pleasant way to get to a restaurant. You can start out as a driver, which usually involves paying a fee or percentage to the pedicab owner, or you can buy your own bicycle taxi and keep all the profits. Until recently these services were found only in the larger metropolitan areas and a few popular tourist destinations, but now you can find bicycle taxis in at least 50 cities across the country.

A good bike is geared so you can easily pedal up small hills even when fully loaded. Although regular taxi companies sometimes lobby local governments to make laws against bicycle taxis, or to regulate them, they are still unregulated in many places. Some cities require a permit, but it is usually inexpensive. In San Diego, for example, the pedicab permit fee is $25.

Money

In larger cities you can simply work as a driver. One New York City company charges 20 percent of fares collected and claims its drivers make $30 to $40 per hour. It is also common for drivers to pay a set fee and keep all receipts. San Diego VIP Pedicab, for example, charges a daily rental fee, which includes liability insurance. It provides free training and claims the typical ride is $10 to $20.

If you start your own company, you have other potential revenue sources. Advertising on the sides of pedicabs generates hundreds of dollars monthly for some companies. Others charge for distributing fliers to the public. Some deliver packages. Of course, you can also buy more pedicabs and hire drivers.

But even as a one-man fare-only operation, you can make a decent wage. The most common rate is $1 per minute, with a $5 minimum. Find four hours of work daily and you'll collect $240 plus tips, for a gross revenue of at least $62,000 annually. Most of that should be profit.

If your town has enough potential and you don't want the physical labor, buy six or more bicycle taxis and rent them out to young people who are social and want to make extra cash. Rental fees are as high as $40 daily in some cities, but even at half of that you can make several thousand dollars monthly on your investment.

How to Get Started

Being a driver for an existing company can pay well. It's a good way to start and to learn the business. Study up on the history of the city and points of interest. For your own business, you'll need a pedicab. They cost $2,000 to $4,000 new and about half of that used. Ask at city hall about regulations and permits. You'll need liability insurance, which can cost several hundred dollars annually. With insurance, a permit, a few business cards, and a used bicycle taxi, this is a business you can start for less than $2,000.

Resources

- *Bike Repair and Maintenance For Dummies* by Dennis Bailey and Keith Gates (Wiley Publishing, 2009): Learn how to keep your equipment working.
- www.biketaxi.net: An example of a bicycle-taxi service in South Carolina.
- www.pedicab.com: Pedicabs, parts, and supplies. Click the "operators" link for great information on starting a bicycle taxi business.
- www.ibike.org/economics/pedicab-intl.htm: You can find links to pedicab companies around the world here, to see how others do it.

CHAPTER 19

YOUR PRODUCT COST IS ZERO

WORM GRUNTING AND FARMING

People buy worms for two reasons. They're sold by the dozen at sporting goods stores and gas stations across the country for fishing bait, and they are sold by the pound for use in gardens and compost bins. Whether red worms, common garden worms, or night crawlers, they all work for both purposes. Some customers even seek worm poop (more often called vermicast or worm castings), which is used as an organic fertilizer and soil conditioner.

The lowest-cost way to get into the worm business is to collect them. Worm grunting, also called worm fiddling, involves pounding a wooden stake called a *stob* into the ground in rich woods and rubbing a *rooping iron* across the top of it, creating vibrations that can cause thousands of worms to exit the ground within a 30-foot area. Pick them up, pack them, and ship them out. Try this business and you can make your trip to the Sopchoppy Worm Grunting Festival in Florida a business write-off. Other options include collecting night crawlers on dewy summer nights, searching for worms in leaf piles, and digging for them. Invest in bins and other equipment, and you can farm worms to sell both to gardening and fishing customers.

Money

Fishing worms and night crawlers retail for $3 to $5 per dozen, and you'll likely get half of that wholesaling them to small shops. Minimum orders and well-planned routes are necessary to make this business efficient. Your profit margins will obviously be higher if you collect rather than farm worms, but time has to be considered. Worms are bought in larger quantities by bait shops and gardeners for about $25 to $35 per pound, plus shipping. There are typically 400 night crawlers in a pound, and closer to 1,000 red worms or garden worms.

In an article in the *Miami Herald,* worm grunter Gary Revell said he does about 200 roops (stob placements) daily and gets "from a handful to 5,000 worms a roop." He wouldn't discuss business details, other than to say he sells the worms for about 6 cents each and pays a permit fee for working on state forest lands. David and Diane Monroe, who now sell vermiculture (worm farming) products on Ecologytek.com, say they made more than $30,000 their first year farming worms, working part-time. Their second year they did $139,936 working full-time.

How to Get Started

If you live in a good fishing area, you can collect worms and sell them by the dozen at docks and boat launches. In Michigan I've seen thousands of worms come out onto the sidewalks and streets to avoid drowning after a heavy rain. In circumstances like that, you might collect and sell hundreds of dollars' worth in a few hours. For consistent profits, though, you'll need to either live near areas of the Southeast where worm grunting is viable, or become a worm farmer. You'll also need to sell wholesale. Check bait shops and other potential buyers to see what you can charge, and track your expenses and time carefully at first to see how much you are making for your time.

Resources

- www.wormdigest.org: Everything you want to know about worms.
- www.jamesmaurer.com/worm-grunting.asp: A worm-grunting article and video.
- www.ecologytek.com: Information on starting a worm farm, equipment, and they'll buy your worms wholesale.
- www.wormfarmingsecrets.com: Information on selling worm castings.
- www.earthworms4sale.com: An example of an online worm seller.

PART THREE

DIRTY AND UGLY JOBS

Perhaps the ugliest way I made money was at age 14, when I discovered I could retrieve stacks of pornographic magazines from newspaper recycling bins near our house and sell them for a dollar each at school. My dirtiest job later in life was being a live-in babysitter (is there a masculine term for nanny?) because I had to change the diapers of babies whose diet was largely grape Kool-Aid. Sometime after that I made $1,700 in 10 or 12 months, collecting sticky pop cans four hours weekly to return for the deposit (10 cents each). And I definitely got dirty when I worked in a small factory drilling holes in muffler brackets (I quit after three days).

The allure of dirty and ugly ways to make money isn't in the dirt or ugliness—unless you have a very strange psychology. Nasty work can be interesting, but the biggest reason for doing the dirtier work is that it is often more profitable because of the lack of competition. After all, the only reason crime-scene cleaners can charge as much as $600 per hour in some areas is that not many people want to scrub blood and guts off of floors and walls. And did you know that some New York City garbage collectors make more than $100,000 annually? Read on . . .

ERIC AND MELINDA JOHNSON, MELRICS MOBILE LUBE

Eric and Melinda Johnson started Melrics Mobile Lube in 1999. In 2002 they created their *How to Start a Mobile Oil Change Business Manual*. Although they recently closed their oil-change business for health reasons, they continue to update the manual as needed so that they can help others get started. I asked Melinda for a bit of their history and some advice for those who might want a mobile oil change business.

What led you to start a mobile oil-change business?

Eric was a supervisor on salary [means being paid for 40 hours but worked up to 80]. I was an hourly worker and overtime was required. We always had a ton of "to-do" items on our list that we couldn't find time to do. Of course most things just kept getting put off because we simply didn't have the time. We wanted to start a business that would help others in the same "no time" boat as we were in. After much searching, we heard of one company that offered on-site oil change services. We kicked that idea around and mentioned it to various friends, family, and coworkers, and everyone thought it was an excellent idea!

Did you start part-time, or did you jump in and go full-time immediately?

We went into it full-time; however, we made a lot of costly mistakes. Paying too much for product, and advertising in the wrong places, etc. . . . So we did go back to work at the same company we had previously worked at. . . . Eric only worked about two months; I stayed on for another three months. At that time we had built up enough to go back to running the business and sleep nights again.

How many oil changes can a one-person operation typically do in a week?

At first . . . I'd suggest you give yourself 45 minutes per vehicle. Once you have been at it a while and provided all vehicles are in one or two locations, you can easily service 10 to 14 vehicles in a normal day. Working five days a week, you should be able to service 50 to 70 vehicles. . . . We have had weeks where we also had evening accounts, so we might start at 8 AM servicing fleets or employee sign-up accounts and then at 6 PM start on an evening fleet account, finishing up around midnight! On those days we have serviced over 20 vehicles.

What other products and services can be offered profitably?

Tire rotations—those cost you nothing but your time. Air-filter and wiper-blade replacement are good choices. Serpentine belts are very profitable; however, there are some vehicles that have the motor mount in the way so you simply cannot provide serpentine-belt replacement for all vehicles.

How much money does it take to get started in this business?

There are several companies that build mobile oil-change systems. . . . Consider a range of $6,000 to $12,000 for a decent new system. . . . You will also have your office supplies, phone, business cards, brochures, etc. Business insurance is a must-have also. . . . For a ballpark figure, $20,000 to $40,000 would be a fair guess.

How can a person learn the necessary skills?

You do not need any automotive training courses. If you know how to change your oil and perform basic maintenance, then you can do this. It does help to be a "people person," meaning that you can go out and talk to potential customers. This is not a business where you place an ad and customers flock to you. You have to go talk to those potential customers in order to build a customer base.

Do you have any other advice?

It can be a very good business if it suits you. Just make sure that it does! Consider that you will be out in the elements. . . . If you are extremely shy and cannot talk to strangers . . . this is not the business for you! Make sure that you do your homework . . . find out all the expenses . . . complete a break-even worksheet to make sure that this will be profitable. . . . Above all, this is not a get-rich-quick business; it does take time to build up a customer base. After you have considered everything and if it still sounds like a good plan for you—go for it!

CHAPTER 20

JIMINY CRICKET!

CRICKET-FARMER

Frogs, lizards, salamanders, and turtles eat crickets, and owners of these pets do not generally want to catch their own. They typically buy the insects online and have them shipped to them, or they get their crickets at a local pet store. Fishermen also use crickets, buying them at bait shops or sporting goods stores. Some of the biggest buyers are zoos and theme parks with reptiles, including Disney's Animal Kingdom, SeaWorld, and Busch Gardens. As a cricket farmer, then, your customers can be the public, the retailers, and big users like zoos and animal sanctuaries.

Cricket farming can be noisy, and sometimes a bit smelly, and the little ones inevitably escape, according to those in the business. On the other hand, it can be a simple, inexpensive business to start. And it *can* be profitable. Cricket paralysis virus (CPV) is in the news at the moment and has caused some cricket farms to close completely. Check the latest news online by searching "cricket virus." As I write this, most farms are shipping product, while some are shutting down for cleaning but planning to reopen soon. The good news is that this has created a cricket shortage, which almost guarantees you can sell all that you can produce, and at better prices.

Money

At the moment, live adult crickets sell for about $8 to $12 for 250, plus shipping, and are mailed out in various containers. In volume they sell much cheaper, with at least one online site advertising 10,000 crickets for $160 in 10 boxes of 1,000 each. Prices are expected to rise if more farms are affected by the cricket paralysis virus. Large orders are where the money is of course. Central Florida Zoo, for example, buys 13,000 crickets weekly for its toads, frogs, geckos, and salamanders. Armstrong Cricket Farms, in Georgia and Louisiana, ship out 17 million crickets per week.

Some cricket farms employ up to 30 people. At least two have been around for more than 50 years. Manta.com estimates that Ghann's Cricket Farm makes between $10 million and $20 million annually and lists others with estimated revenues of $1 million to $5 million.

How to Get Started

You can search online for a cricket farm near you if you want to start as an employee. That would give you some experience and a feel for whether you like the business. If it is a large operation, you might just see if you can get a tour and then ask a lot of questions while you are there.

This business is a relatively easy one to start for a couple of hundred dollars. Aquariums, garbage cans, and plastic tubs are used for breeding by small-scale producers. Food and starter crickets are cheap. Once you get some experience, you'll need to scale up to make a decent profit. Also, because of the danger of losing all your crickets to a virus, it might be best to emulate those businesses that in addition to raising crickets, also farm red worms, mealworms, hissing cockroaches, and other critters (now you know how shock television shows get the bugs they make contestants eat). If you're going to get dirty anyhow, you might as well diversify for safety.

Resources

- www.breeding-crickets.com: Information on cricket farming.
- www.flukerfarms.com: A cricket farm that sells supplies.
- www.ghann.com: This cricket farm appeared on Mike Rowe's *Dirty Jobs* television show.
- www.anapsid.org/crickets.html: A cricket breeding guide and low-cost cricket-food recipe.

CHAPTER 21

MOPPING UP BRAINS

CRIME-SCENE CLEANER

The owner of a carpet-cleaning company I once worked for considered getting into crime-scene cleanup. I wasn't thrilled about cleaning up blood and skull fragments, but I probably would have done it (the owner changed his mind). Most people don't plan to get into this line of work but come from related fields. Ambulance drivers, for example, or house cleaners see the income potential and start a crime-scene-cleanup business or get hired by one.

CTS Decon—crime and trauma scene decontamination—involves wearing a hot biohazard suit for hours as you clean up methamphetamine labs, anthrax-exposure sites, and, naturally, the sites of violent crimes and suicides. Most people do not move after a murder or suicide takes place in their home, so the job of a crime-scene cleaner is to erase all signs of what happened. A sympathetic nature helps, but you also need a strong stomach and a bit of detachment. You'll rip out stained carpeting, clean up decomposing remains of murder victims (the coroner takes only the big pieces), wash blood off windows, and more.

Money

Crime-scene cleaners start at about $30,000 annually in most areas. In large cities with lots of crime, it is possible to make more than $75,000. To make more than that, you'll normally have to own the business. Do your homework before starting, paying particular attention to how existing companies get their clients. Some newer companies claim that the police play favorites in many cities, pushing grieving families to use companies that may pay kickbacks or be owned by friends. Normal charges are from $100 to $600 per hour, so even small cleaning jobs can generate thousands of dollars.

How to Get Started

Although there are some educational services that train you for this work, at this point most employees are trained on the job. Bio-technicians, as cleaners are often called, need to be in good shape (you will have to carry bloody mattresses and tear open walls at times) and have a stable personality. Your employer should pay for you to get the hepatitis B vaccine, and most will require that you get certified for handling hazardous materials. At the moment, CTS Decon companies are hiring in many parts of the country. One lists four field technician openings and has an online application. It requires 24/7 availability (crimes happen day and night), willingness to travel, good health, and the ability to work as a team with others. Interestingly, it also prefers applicants with construction experience.

Working as an employee is definitely recommended prior to starting a business in this field, unless you are already in a general cleaning business. Though you can operate a crime-scene-cleanup company from home, some substantial investments are still necessary, such as a van, an ozone machine for odors, and cleaning equipment of various types. The industry isn't regulated nationally (check at the state level), but you have to follow guidelines established by the Occupational Safety and Health Administration for handling biohazardous materials, as well as any state rules.

Resources

- *Mop Men: Inside the World of Crime Scene Cleaners* by Alan Emmins (Thomas Dunne Books, 2009).
- http://science.howstuffworks.com/crime-scene-clean-up.htm: Several pages of good information.
- www.actremediation.com: A crime-scene-cleanup company in Wisconsin.
- www.crimeclean-up.net: A crime-scene-cleanup company that also offers education and training in the field.
- www.keybusinessideas.com/crime-scene-cleanup.html: Information and an inexpensive course on how to start a crime-scene-cleanup company.

CHAPTER 22

PUMPING POOP

SEPTIC CLEANER

According to the Environmental Protection Agency, nearly one in four households in the United States depends on an individual septic system or community cluster system. That's about 20 to 30 million septic tanks in the country, and they all fill with sludge on the bottom and floating material on the surface of the liquid inside. If not pumped out regularly, these systems fail, sewage backs up into the home, and major repairs and cleanup are required.

When my own septic system was pumped years ago, I watched from a distance and talked to the employee operating the vacuum hose. He was very careful, but splashes still occurred. It's a nasty job, to say the least, and it includes cleaning and rinsing the walls of the underground septic tank. He had five cleanings scheduled that day. He finished mine in about an hour, but it was an easy one.

Money

When a service is necessary yet few people want to provide it, wages or profits are usually higher than average. In this case, making a bit more than fast-food employees may not be exciting given the nature of the work, but employment can provide the knowledge necessary to start your own business. The latest statistics show average wages for septic tank cleaners are about $29,000 annually, although a fourth of them make more than $35,000 annually.

As the owner, expect to charge between $200 to $500 per job depending on local competition, regulations, and access to septic tank covers (which are often buried). The big money—and the satisfaction of no longer pumping the poop yourself—comes when you hire employees and run several trucks. A single septic-pumping truck can easily produce more than

$1,000 daily in revenue, and dozens of multitruck companies exceed $5 million in annual revenues.

How to Get Started

The U.S. Bureau of Labor Statistics projects faster-than-average job growth in this field. Check classified job listings, but it's common for septic-cleaning companies to have unadvertised openings. Look in local yellow pages under "Septic Tanks and Systems: Cleaning and Repair," or "Sewer Cleaners." Experience is rarely a requirement—you'll be trained on the job.

If you're looking at employment as a step toward your own business, take notes as you work. Ask the owner about all the local regulations, the equipment, and the other costs. As I prepared this chapter, a quick check online showed numerous used septic pumpers for sale—trucks with the necessary vacuum equipment and 2,000-gallon tanks. Prices ranged from $4,000 to $70,000. It is not a low-cost business to start, but it's possible for many people using a home equity loan to finance a start-up.

Resources

- *Small Business For Dummies* by Eric Tyson and Jim Schell (Wiley Publishing, 2008): A guide to every aspect of starting and growing almost any business.
- www.americanliquidwaste.com: *American Liquid Waste Magazine* provides online information about relevant associations and industry news.
- http://en.wikipedia.org/wiki/Septic_tank: This Wikipedia entry will give you a quick overview of what a septic system is and how it works.
- www.yellowpages.com: Enter "Septic Tanks and Systems" and similar search phrases, with the name of towns in which you prefer to work.

CHAPTER 23

TRAVELING GREASE MONKEY

MOBILE OIL-CHANGER

Why do people want an oil change done at their home or place of business? Convenience. Why might you want to offer this service to them? It's a decent niche with less competition than a fixed-location oil-change business. But there are two other important advantages as well.

First, your initial investment can be much lower. It's true you'll need a van, but you can get a loan for that *and* for a $10,000 oil-change system. Another thousand dollars and you'll have a decent stock of oil and other supplies. A few thousand dollars of your own and you're good to go. Second, your ongoing overhead can be very low. You can operate this business from home, with a cheap second phone line or cell phone. You can also opt for free or low-cost ways to market yourself. Even with the van and equipment payments, your break-even point will be very low. Two jobs daily can be enough to make a profit. That makes this a part-time business that is very low risk but one that can be built into a full-time income.

A warning from those in the field though: It can be a cold and dirty job in the winter. You typically work outdoors, sometimes arranging to do six or more cars at a location (an employee special at a business location, for example), so be prepared.

Money

The web site Locationlube.com estimates annual business expenses of about $50,000 based on 60 oil changes per week. That volume is reasonable according to those in the industry. The expense estimate includes advertising fliers, insurance, finance payments for equipment, telephone, accounting, uniforms, fuel, waste disposal, and cost of goods. Each job, with a $33.95 oil change and extra sales (wiper blades, air filters, tire rotations), should bring in about

$40. Multiply that by 60 jobs per week for 52 weeks and you have a gross revenue of about $125,000, for a net of about $75,000 annually—based on a one-man, one-van operation. With lower expenses (pay cash for equipment to avoid loan payments, for example), your profit could be substantially higher.

If you have employees and they cost 30 percent of total sales, that 60-jobs-per-week average nets you about $38,000 annually for each van operating. Three vans and you are doing six figures without getting dirty.

How to Get Started

Investigate the market to see how many mobile oil-change services are operating in your area, and call to ask how busy they are. If they're doing only a few oil changes daily, there may already be too much competition. Many areas (our hometown included) currently have no mobile lube services, and perhaps room for only one.

The basics of changing oil can be learned relatively quickly. You can watch as they change your oil at a traditional oil-change company, or better yet, call a mobile oil-change service to do the job while you take notes. Working briefly for an oil-change company can help. The companies that sell the complete oil-change systems normally install them in your van for you *and* train you in their use as part of the price.

Resources

- *Mobile Oil Change Company* by Tim Roncevich and Steven Primm (CreateSpace, 2009).
- www.melrics.com: Information on starting a mobile oil-change business.
- www.mobileoilchangeservices.com: An example of a mobile oil-change business.
- www.lubengo.com: A supplier of mobile oil-change systems.
- www.youtube.com: There are a number of videos here on how to change oil.

CHAPTER 24

ANOTHER POOPORTUNITY

DIAPER-CLEANING SERVICE

Cloth or disposable? Studies reported in the *Journal of Pediatrics* suggest that the incidence of diaper rash increased dramatically as paper-and-plastic disposables largely replaced cotton diapers. Some studies indicate cloth diapers can be just as bad if not used properly, but few suggest that cotton is worse. It almost certainly feels better than paper and plastic. For that reason and because of environmental concerns, many parents are returning to cotton. Of course, washing cloth diapers *could be* more work than using disposables, but that's why cloth diaper services exist. Parents just throw dirty diapers in a special container, and they're picked up weekly when clean ones are dropped off. Many families even save money using a diaper service versus the cost of disposable diapers.

Let's recap the benefits: Cloth diapers are more comfortable, cheaper, more environmentally friendly, and healthier. That's your sales pitch, by the way, when you're ready to start your own cloth diaper service. Typically, you charge by the week or month. You run each route weekly, so with one vehicle you can have up to five routes. Drop off clean diapers, pick up dirty ones, wash them, and repeat.

Money

Employees in this field are classified as laundry workers by the Bureau of Labor Statistics, and the average annual wage for this group is $20,790. To make much money with diaper cleaning, clearly you have to own the business. Get a list of new baby births from hospitals if possible, or cross-promote with infant product stores, midwives, and other businesses that deal with new parents. Once you develop a mailing list, send fliers explaining the benefits of your service, or drop them off with a free sample diaper.

A typical charge per baby is $18 weekly. That usually includes 70 or 80 diapers for newborns, or as few as 30 for toddlers. The fee to get set up initially (clients need a diaper containers, etc.) is typically from $25 to $50. If you do most of the work yourself, up to half of your revenue can be profit, which means 160 customers at about $1,000 each annually would give you a profit of $80,000. The business-data site Manta.com lists many diaper services that top $1 million in annual revenue.

How to Get Started

Read up on the basic procedures for properly laundering diapers. Visit web sites of existing services to see how they are operating, what additional services or products they offer, and in particular, what the typical prices are in your area. You may have to call to get the latter, as some companies do not list their prices online. Do some research to determine if enough demand exists in a small enough area to make it profitable (you can't have five-mile drives between customers).

The start-up cost for a diaper service can be as low as $2,000 and up to 10 times that or more. If your budget is at the lower end, you can start without washing machines and dryers. You can drop off and pick up the diapers by contracting with a commercial laundry facility to clean them. Profit margins will be lower, so you'll want to eventually invest in your own machines. Then again, never actually washing the diapers might make this business more attractive, even if it's a bit less profitable.

Resources

- www.realdiaperindustry.org: A trade organization site full of information for those in the cloth diaper industry.
- www.ecobabydiaperservice.com: A Colorado cloth diaper company.
- www.diaperjungle.com: Information on running a cloth diaper business, and links to diaper wholesalers and more.

CHAPTER 25

PREPARING THE WAY FOR SANTA

CHIMNEY SWEEP

In the United States each year, more than 20,000 residential fires originate in chimneys, fireplaces, and wood-fuel furnaces. They result in many deaths and millions in property damage. One of the best ways to prevent those fires is to have chimneys and stovepipes inspected and cleaned regularly. That is the primary job of a chimney sweep.

If you're not afraid of heights, you like to work outdoors, and you don't mind getting dirty, you might do well as a chimney sweep. It is a business that can be started relatively inexpensively, done part time if you want, and yet has the potential to grow. You will be working both in the client's house and up on the roof. The basic equipment starts with a few chimney brushes along with a pole to push and pull them through chimneys and pipes. Other services include inspection of attics and wood heating systems, carbon monoxide testing, and repairs to chimneys and wood stoves. You don't have to wear the traditional top hat, but some do for marketing purposes.

Money

Because only a few thousand people are in the industry, competition is light in many areas, keeping wages relatively high. The labor department lumps chimney sweeps in with brick masons and shows average annual income for employees in this group as $42,000. Probably only a few apprentice positions are available at any given time, but as I write this there are several postings online, including a company hiring in Bellingham, Massachusetts, promising $800 to $1,200 weekly.

Naturally, you have more profit potential as the owner of the business. A typical cleaning is between $75 and $175 depending on the size of the job and the area of the country. Additional services, such as air-quality testing, can add substantially to that. Installing a chimney liner, for example, is typically $1,200. Overhead is low if you operate from home, and equipment and supplies are relatively inexpensive, so as an owner-operator your revenue will be mostly profit, and margins are high enough to hire employees and still make a good profit per job. Recent data shows that dozens of chimney sweeps do more than $1 million in annual revenue and have 10 or more employees. Most of these larger companies provide additional services like chimney repairs and general roof inspections—something to keep in mind if you want to grow your business.

How to Get Started

If you can find a chimney sweep who needs help, that would be a good way to get experience. Otherwise, you can read up on the basic techniques (see the resources below) and practice on your own chimney and those of friends. Although lengthy experience can lead to better skills and knowledge in all the trades, this is a relatively simple one to learn. The Chimney Safety Institute of America (CSIA) offers a certification program by way of a written test. Being a certified chimney sweep can help you get hired and/or help you market yourself as a business. CSIA members get business referrals, too.

Resources

- www.ncsg.org: National Chimney Sweep Guild; good information and the latest industry news.
- www.fireplaceessentials.com: Chimney brushes and other supplies.
- www.chimneycleaners.com: Example of a chimney sweep company.
- http://youtube.com: Search "how to clean a chimney," and you'll find several videos that walk you through the process.
- www.csia.org: Certification program, referrals for members, and loads of good information about the business.

CHAPTER 26

CAPTURING WILD ANIMALS

ANIMAL-CONTROL SPECIALIST

I once had to trap a raccoon that was causing damage. It managed to take the bait and escape the cage twice before I caught it. I'll hire help next time. Most people would rather not deal with animal pests on their own. Pest control companies or exterminators typically go after ants, termites, and rodents. Animal control, also called animal damage control, wildlife control, or nuisance animal control, is a much broader field. Workers in this field help customers who have problems with bats, alligators, coyotes, mice, skunks, raccoons, bees, wasps, woodpeckers, opossums, squirrels, feral dogs, beavers, snakes, chipmunks, armadillos, foxes, seagulls, pigeons, and more.

This is a good job or business for those who like to work outdoors, don't mind getting dirty, and love a challenge. Every job will be a little different, and the nature of the work depends on which animals are the most common pests where you live. You might install screens for one client to prevent animals from getting into a crawl space, and then trap raccoons for the next customer. Pulling alligators out of swimming pools is a possibility if you operate in the South, where snake capture can also be part of the job.

Money

Animal–control specialists (employees) average about $28,000 annually. You can make much more than that as the operator of your own business. A service call can start at $150 for the first 30 minutes, for example. That would typically include an inspection, evaluation, recommendations, and removal of nuisance animals if possible at that time. Return trips are extra, and some companies double rates for holidays and emergencies. Specializing can limit your client base but allow you to charge more. For example, in some areas you might specialize in dangerous animals, like venomous snakes and alligators. In other areas, you might specialize in deer-proofing yards and gardens.

Other revenue sources include prevention measures (special fencing, applying animal repellents), animal-damage repairs, chimney caps, vent screens, attic fan screens, fencing, and screens for crawl spaces. What's the ultimate potential? In recent statistics of companies under the category of "nuisance animal control," at least 80 have estimated annual revenues of more than $1 million.

How to Get Started

Working for an existing company is an excellent way to get trained and learn what you need to know to start your own business. Very few books about this business exist, but you can find a wealth of information online. To get a broad education, do a few dozen searches of "how to get rid of . . ." plus the name of each possible animal pest. If you or your friends have any animal problems, you can practice your new knowledge and skills.

Start-up costs for a nuisance animal control business can vary according to the animals that are a problem in your area and whether you specialize or deal with all of them. Talk to others in the industry to see what you'll need. For this research, approach companies in neighboring towns where you won't be directly competing against them. You can promise to refer clients if you get calls for jobs that are closer to them. Ask about local or state regulations as well.

Resources

- www.aallanimalcontrol.com: A nuisance animal control company that offers franchises.
- www.bird-x.com: A supplier of animal pest control products.
- www.animalcontrolspecialists.com: A company based in Illinois.
- http://raccoon-x.com: Products for and information about getting rid of raccoons.

CHAPTER 27

CLEAN UP WITH THIS DIRTY JOB

GARBAGE AND JUNK HAULER

Wheel that garbage bin to the truck, hook it up, pull the lever to dump it in the compactor, and pick up the potato peelings and diapers that escape and fall at your feet. Collecting garbage is truly dirty work. Why do it? Because you don't need a degree, you get to work outside, and it can pay better than you might think.

You've seen garbage collectors doing their jobs, and there isn't that much more than what you see (no offense to those in the field, but this is not one of the more highly skilled professions). You can be trained on the job in a few days or a week, and with additional training and licensing become a garbage truck driver to earn even more. And then there is the possibility of owning your own general trash collection company, or specializing in one of the junk-hauling niches.

Money

Garbage collectors, called *refuse and recyclable material collectors* in Labor Department statistics, average $33,760 per year. CNN recently reported on New York City trash collectors who make more than $100,000 annually thanks to a strong union and overtime pay. That high pay results in high prices, which creates opportunities for entrepreneurs. Some find they can easily compete against the big players using just a pickup truck to start and charging substantially less than the going rates (see the resources section for a blog post that details one example of this). Most towns no longer grant monopolies to big trash haulers, so this plan can work in areas where existing services are expensive.

There is less competition in a niche like junk cleanup and hauling. With a pickup truck and a good back, you're in business, and cleaning junk out of a garage or hauling old furniture is somewhat cleaner work than regular trash collection. A typical charge is $65 for a single item or $150 for a pickup truck load. The latter can be dumped for $30 at many landfills, leaving a decent profit, especially if you do several jobs daily. Another niche is cleaning up and hauling away construction site debris. Manta.com lists many junk-hauling companies that top $500,000 in annual revenue.

How to Get Started

It can be tough to get into the high-paying union jobs in larger cities but perhaps worth the effort given the wages. In smaller towns, these jobs are much easier to get and almost always pay more than other jobs that don't require a college education. Small independent companies are the easiest places to get hired, and although their wages tend to be lower, you might use such a job as a step toward getting hired by a municipal waste department.

You can start a trash-collection or junk-hauling service using a pickup truck with high sides and invest in larger trucks when the business grows. Determine your likely fuel costs, dumping costs, truck maintenance, liability insurance, and licensing costs. See what others are charging. To grow, you have to be able to charge a price that makes a profit even when an employee is driving the truck.

Resources

- www.indeed.com: Search "waste management" for thousands of current job listings, including some that pay over $100,000 annually.
- www.junkawayhaulinginc.com: An example of a junk-hauling company.
- www.wm.com/careers/index.jsp: Waste Management operates across the country and posts job openings on its site.
- http://globaleconomicanalysis.blogspot.com/2010/04/trash-collecting-entrepreneur-squashed.html: A great (and sad) story of a man starting a profitable trash collection business charging a third of the going rate.

CHAPTER 28

WORK IN A SEWER

WASTEWATER-TREATMENT WORKER

On good days, wastewater- or sewage-treatment workers will monitor the liquids as they flow through the system. They'll work with manual and computerized equipment and make minor repairs or adjustments. Then there are the days when they have to go into the sewers to remove objects blocking the grates or to replace seals or pump bearings. This means wading knee-deep into a soup of human waste and other nasty components, with the inevitable splashes, as well as dropped tools that have to be searched for in the muck.

Why would you want a career in wastewater treatment? Some workers like the team spirit such dirty jobs inspire. Job security is another benefit, since few people really want to take your position. And the pay can be pretty good. There are niche opportunities as well. Some large prisons have wastewater facilities, for example, and cruise ships also treat sewage before dumping the treated remains in the ocean. There are worse places to work than out at sea on a beautiful ship.

Money

Wastewater-treatment employees average $41,580 annually in the United States, but the average for California and Nevada tops $57,000. New York City's 1,100 sewage treatment workers do even better. Their most recent contract brings the average hourly wage up to $35, with senior sewage-treatment workers making over $38 per hour. Dozens of senior stationary engineers make $50.39 to $53.99 per hour—over $100,000 annually plus benefits. The sewage-treatment departments of many smaller communities are not unionized, and jobs there tend to pay less. On the other hand, the cost of living is also lower in many of those same places. At the moment, searching the employment web site Indeed.com for "wastewater treatment" yields more than a thousand jobs that pay $70,000 or higher annually, and more than 100 that top $110,000. The latter are primarily management positions (perhaps something to aim for).

How to Get Started

Some positions have relatively minimal requirements and you'll get most of your training on the job. For example, one position, advertised online at the moment requires only a high school diploma, driver's license, and a test (with a $35 fee for taking it). The employer does prefer that applicants have experience in a related field, which could be as a septic-system cleaner, or work in plumbing. Starting pay is $31,000 annually, with advancement to $48,000 after two years and completion of several wastewater-treatment courses.

Employers often require certifications. These, and the courses needed for them, are usually meant for work in a particular state (an example can be found in the resources section). Call local wastewater-treatment facilities to ask what they require and where you can get the necessary training or education. If you find that experience in related fields is a common requirement, you might consider working for a septic-tank cleaning company for some months while you apply for wastewater-treatment positions. Some niches may be easier to get into, like the prison or cruise-ship positions mentioned earlier.

Resources

- *Water and Wastewater Treatment: A Guide for the Nonengineering Professionals* by Joanne Drinan (CRC Press, 2000).
- www.cpe.vt.edu/wwplant: A certification provider for workers in wastewater treatment.
- www.indeed.com: Search "wastewater treatment" and you'll find thousands of job postings across the country.
- http://en.wikipedia.org/wiki/Sewage_treatment: The whole process of wastewater treatment is explained here.

CHAPTER 29

PERHAPS THE STINKIEST JOB?

MAGGOT FARMER

The Porthill Maggot Farm is known for an almost unbearable odor of ammonia. You may have seen it profiled on Mike Rowe's *Dirty Jobs* program on the Discovery Channel. Rowe helped with feeding, then scooped up and packaged thousands of squirming maggots in the processing plant. The maggots eat up ground-up fish and other foods almost as fast as they can be shoveled into their feeding bins. Then there are the flies that have to be bred to lay the eggs that become the maggots. If you're not getting excited about this work yet, perhaps I should add that Pam and Dennis Ponsness, the owners of the farm, sell and ship three to four million maggots weekly.

Maggots are sold as fishing bait. Bluebottle fly larvae are bought by the millions, then hatched to pollinate certain crops. The Porthill Farm has had big orders from USDA research stations, as well as crime movies and television shows. They once shipped several hundred thousand maggots to the Brooklyn Museum of Art. Those were used in a controversial art display. This is not an operation you can run if you live near people, but if you live out of town and don't mind working in an environment of buzzing flies, horrible stench, and millions of swarming maggots, this might be the business for you.

Money

Bluebottle larvae are typically sold by the cup (about 1,700 maggots per cup) as pollinators. Prices vary according to order size. The Forked Tree Ranch in Idaho, for example, currently sells them for $10.45 per cup with a 3-cup minimum, or as cheaply as $6.30 per cup for orders of 32 cups or more.

Black soldier fly larvae are another common maggot, usually referred to as soldier grubs. A favorite of fishermen, they typically sell for about $16, including shipping, for a cup of 500. They are also sold as food for pond fish, chickens, and reptiles and for use in compost bins (they devour almost any-thing). Be sure to remind your customers to keep the maggots refrigerated prior to use so they do not develop into flies.

The potential profits are difficult to estimate in small niche markets like this. The Porthill Maggot Farm is doing well. Maggot farmers are commonly worm farmers as well, and several worm farms in the United States have gross revenues of more than $500,000 annually.

How to Get Started

I recently watched a video of some very happy employees working at a maggot farm, but there really aren't that many positions out there, and the money is clearly in being the owner of the business. A visit to a maggot farm (or worm farm if there are no maggot sellers in your area) is a good place to start your education. It may be best to begin your venture with black soldier fly larvae because the profit margins are higher, so you are more likely to be able to start on a small scale. Starter kits are available online (see the resources section), and the basic equipment is inexpensive.

Resources

- www.youtube.com/watch?v=KPU5DE0Z_TA: A video covering the maggot-farming process at a 30-year business, with short interviews of employees.
- http://en.wikipedia.org/wiki/Maggot: A nice article about maggots, de-scribing their use by fishermen and in healing open wounds.
- www.thewormdude.com: Grub (maggot) starter kits and bins designed for raising them.
- www.speedyworm.com/spikes.htm: An example of a maggot seller.
- www.interstellar-solutions.co.uk/Maggot_Farming_Business_Plan.html: A business plan for maggot farmers.

CHAPTER 30

BLOOD-SUCKING PROFITS

LEECHES

When I was young, I would explore ponds and swamps, and sometimes come out with four or five leeches on my legs. Having just checked a site that sells these little bloodsuckers, I now know that I had $50 hanging from my legs. That's right, leeches sell for as much as $12 each . . . or as cheaply as 20 cents. It all depends on the species. The cheap ones are used as fishing bait and are usually trapped. You get to work outdoors if you start a bait-leech business.

Medicinal leeches are bred. Common species used include *Hirudo medicinalis*, *Hirudo orientalis*, *Hirudo verbana*, *Hirudinaria manillensis*, and *Macrobdella decora*. First used in medicine more than 200 years ago, then largely forgotten for a time, leech therapy is becoming popular once again. Leeches are used in microsurgery to reduce blood coagulation and are used to stimulate circulation in reattachment operations for eyelids, fingers, and other body parts. The anticoagulant hirudin, found in leeches, can't be harvested efficiently, so it is expected that there will be a market for live leeches for some time to come.

Money

It's always tricky to estimate the profit potential of new niche businesses, and that's especially true in the case of medicinal leech sales. Leech therapy, also known as hirudotherapy, was just approved for use in the United States in 2004. It *is* gaining in popularity. Dr. Harry Hoyen, a hand surgeon at Metro-Health in Cleveland, Ohio, estimates that he uses leeches in 10 percent of his finger-reattachment surgeries, for example. The National Health Service in England buys 50,000 bloodsuckers annually. Typically, medicinal leeches sell for $7 or $12 each, plus shipping.

If you want to get into the business of bait leeches, which means trapping rather than farming, expect to sell them for about $20 to $35 per pound based on size and quantity ordered. A pound usually includes 100 to 200 leeches.

How to Get Started

More information is available about leech trapping than about farming medicinal leeches. In fact, you can watch many good videos online showing trappers doing their work.

If you're interested in selling medicinal leeches to hospitals, set aside a space where you won't be bothered by the odor, which has been likened to stale meat. The odor becomes especially strong when they are fed, after which they urinate for several days. The good news is that once they reach the appropriate size, you no longer need to feed them, as they can live for up to a year without food. The bad news is that since this is still a relatively new industry, it is unclear if you will be facing new regulations or if hospitals will feel comfortable buying from a novice leech farmer. In fact, just two businesses currently supply most U.S. hospitals, and their leeches come from certified breeding facilities located overseas. This suggests that you might be better off leaving the farming to others and just starting a leech importation and distribution business.

Resources

- www.agromedic.com: Sellers of a medicinal-leech breeding kit.
- www.jewelloutdoors.com/leeches.html: Sellers of leeches for fishing bait.
- www.youtube.com: Search "leech trapping" and you'll find several good how-to videos.
- www.leeches.biz: Information on medicinal leeches and a seller of leeches.
- www.leechesusa.com: One of the larger medicinal leech sellers in the United States.

PART FOUR

INTERNET OPPORTUNITIES

Years ago a friend told me he made $600 monthly online from pay-per-click advertising. People clicked on ads and he got paid. Making only $600 per month from clicks would be depressing now, but at the time it was exciting. My wife and I wanted a business we could take with us as we moved around the country looking for a place to settle down. I hated computers, but soon I learned to tolerate them, and I love writing. Now, with more than three dozen web sites, we make money from pay-per-click revenue, e-books, affiliate commissions, royalties on Amazon Kindle books, and other online ventures.

From speculating in virtual real estate to giving away e-books, this section will cover some of the more interesting ways you can use the Internet to make some extra cash or make a living or even get rich. You can get paid sharing your expertise (and we're all experts on something), or testing products and reporting your results on a review site. You can even make money sitting in a cabin on Lake Baikal in Siberia with your laptop, writing short blog posts or articles.

MISTER X, DOMAIN-NAME INVESTOR

I've known this particular domain-name investor for years. Preferring to keep a low profile, he didn't want his name used. He has bought and sold Internet domain names for more than 10 years. I can tell you that he is being modest about his success in his answers to my questions. In fact, shortly after this interview he sold two domain names in a week for a total of about $40,000.

How did you get started?

In the late '90s I read a story in World *magazine (www.worldmag.com) about the country of Tonga opening up its allotment of "country code" (.to) domain names for sale to anyone worldwide. I registered one for a business venture in which I was involved and had a small web site built that we listed in the yellow pages.*

71

By now, obviously valuable names like flowers.com are long gone. What do you look for these days in names that you buy?

Potential demand. While no one is going to be interested in buying Super DuperMegaPlusMall.net, someone may however be interested in the simpler and easy to remember MegaMall.com. . . . If you are trying to make money with a web site about Myrtle Beach, South Carolina, you are much better off owning MyrtleBeach.com than VisitMyrtleBeachForAGreatVacation.com, even if it is a catchy phrase. MyrtleBeach.com is much simpler, easier to remember, and easier to type in the browser on your computer. By the way, that developed web site was sold in a multimillion-dollar deal in 2010.

Do you invest in extensions such as .org or .info, or only in .com names?

In the domainer community you will often hear .com is king. True, but alternate extensions can also be valuable. A short .net or .org can be worth much more than a longer, unpronounceable .com. . . . My portfolio is overwhelmingly .com; however, there are some shorter .nets and .orgs that I own and that I have sold.

How long do you typically hold a name, and what do you do with it while you wait?

Oftentimes, years. . . . Others buy and sell quite quickly, constantly marketing the names to have a higher turnover, sacrificing price. . . . I do some outbound marketing, but in most cases, buyers find me. Think about it. If I approach a buyer, it appears I need to sell. If a buyer approaches me, I know that he wants to buy. Pricing power in that case is more in my hands. . . . Many of my names are parked with a domain-parking service. . . . The revenue that results from clicks on advertisers that show up on the page is shared with the domain owner, and there is often a link to find out about purchasing the domain.

What is the most you have paid for a domain name, and what do you typically pay?

It would be rare for me to pay more than a couple thousand dollars for a name. Usually my modus operandi is to find names that might fetch several hundred dollars or more that have lapsed, and purchase them for 10 bucks. One opportunity I have not exploited as much as I could is contacting current owners of domains that are not being used and offering a reasonable (wholesale) amount of money. I've done that a few times and gotten some good names.

What is the most you have sold a domain name for?

Have sold several for tens of thousands of dollars each. My average selling price is around $2,000.

How many domain names do you currently own?
Thousands—less than 10,000.

Great names can be tough to find inexpensively now. Can you suggest at least one way to find decent names at reasonable prices?

Look up the owners of names that are inactive. If you've typed in a web site name that you think should have some content on it, and instead received a "page not found" error, contact the owner. Use the whois lookup on one of the registrar's sites and get a phone number and an e-mail. Remember, too, with spam filters, your e-mail may hit the junk file. Call them. Tell them you are interested and make a reasonable, but not overly generous, offer for the name. Then, if you get it, contact potential buyers. Try to get the .com of a name and resell it for more to the holder of the .net who runs his business on the lesser name.

CHAPTER 31

A LAPTOP IN BANGKOK

SELLING WRITING SERVICES FROM ANYWHERE

I once wrote 110 mini-articles in eight hours, which we posted on a network of blogs to promote our web sites. Each was about 120 words, targeted one keyword, and provided simple tips or information. For example, if the keyword phrase was "brain foods," I had two lines of introduction and a list of a few good foods, with "brain foods" linked to my brainpower web site. Others had backpacking tips and were linked to my backpacking sites. These were top-of-my-head pieces, with only the occasional minute or two of research online.

If that sounds like something you can do—even if at a slower pace—you can make money from anywhere in the world. When I next needed short blog posts, I went to Elance.com and paid a young American living in Singapore $190 to do 100 for me. He finished the job in a couple of days. For short articles (400 to 700 words), I've paid up to $20, and some writers charge $40. Many of us who make a living online don't have time to do all of our own writing, and some just don't want to write. Short articles are bought and distributed to promote web sites, or as page content. Other writing project requests you'll find on the freelance web sites include newsletters, sales pages, speeches, press releases, entire e-books, and translation work.

Money

Your profits depend on skill, speed, and your ability to market yourself. Online businesses can buy short articles for $4 each, but most don't because they're written by people who barely speak English, and it shows. Native English writers get up to $40 for articles and web-page content (400 to 700 words), but $15 is more typical, so efficiency matters. If you write fast, you can make $20 per hour while living in some exotic part of the world where rent is only $200 per month.

For bigger money, learn and focus on niches like copywriting (writing sales pages and promotional mailings) or press release writing. Fees vary greatly, but when I recently requested a quote for a new sales page for one of our sites, I was told by the copywriter that he no longer did anything for less than $5,000. If you know another language, you can do translations of web content and e-books, and expect to get at least $30 per hour.

How to Get Started

Write. With practice you can probably produce informative articles, web pages, or blog posts faster than you think. When I first wrote an article to promote a web site, it took me three hours. Now I crank them out in 30 to 40 minutes. Some writers can do an article in 20 minutes. You need samples to market yourself anyhow, so write a few how-to articles on topics you're familiar with, and a few more on randomly chosen topics that each require five minutes of online research. After you do a dozen, time the next ones to see if you are getting quick enough to make a decent hourly wage. With that practice and your new portfolio, you're ready to begin marketing your services.

Oh, and you'll need a laptop if you plan to travel the world while you do this.

Resources

- *Content Rich: Writing Your Way to Wealth on the Web* by John Wuebben (Encore Publishing, 2008).
- http://999articles.com: My own e-book, *You Can Make Money Writing*, is here, along with a few free excerpts.
- www.elance.com: One of the best places online for getting freelance work.
- www.guru.com: Another good freelance marketplace.

CHAPTER 32

GET RICH WITH
UNREAL ESTATE

VIRTUAL WORLDS

If you've participated in online games like *RuneScape* and *Second Life*, you know you can buy real estate, start a business to earn gold coins, and do many other things that you might want to do in real life. You can also make actual profits speculating in land or building whole fantasy neighborhoods where you sell or rent out homes for real dollars. Catherine Winters, in her book *Second Life: The Official Guide*, says thousands of players dabble in real estate speculation, "and many Second Life people make it a permanent side occupation that delivers a steady stream of profits."

Wired.com recently reported on a virtual castle that sold online for more than $2,000 in real money. It was on a hill on the coast of Britannia, a world that exists only in the game *Ultima Online*. In a study of real estate sales in Norrath, the fantasy world for players of Sony Online's *EverQuest* game, an economist determined the online world had a gross national product of $135 million, which on a per-capita basis equaled the GNP of Bulgaria.

Money

Can you get rich? Ailin Graef was on the cover of *BusinessWeek* after becoming the first person to become a real-world millionaire from her *Second Life* avatar's activities. She was making $150,000 annually and had holdings in the online game that could be sold for over a million dollars in real money. Spending just $9.95 to start, she used Anshe Chung, her online avatar, to buy virtual land, which she subdivided and developed for resale. She also rented out some properties. This was built into a virtual empire in time.

Selling and renting houses is just a start. Companies are advertising in virtual worlds, making prime locations for virtual billboards very valuable. Smart players started buying up the best virtual real estate a few years back, but it isn't too late to get in on the profits. If you really want to think out of the box, look for new ways to tap into this billion-dollar market. Maybe you'll be the first mortgage lender to loan on virtual real estate.

How to Get Started

A credit card and Internet access is all you need. Many online role-playing games have free registration, but you'll need a premium account to do business properly. These usually cost less than $10 monthly. Read the rules before signing up, and visit forums where players discuss the games. Go to Ebay.com and other auction sites to see what virtual land, game money, and other items from these virtual worlds are selling for.

Online worlds with the most players usually have the greatest appreciation in virtual real estate values. You may have to participate for several weeks to see how much work it will be to accumulate game-world currency, the "money" that will buy the in-world real estate. Compare the potential profits and the time required in the case of each world. You want the maximum return for your time in real dollar terms.

Resources

- http://en.wikipedia.org/wiki/Massively_multiplayer_online_role-playing_game: A good overview of MMORPGs (massively multiplayer online role-playing games).
- http://secondlife.com: Click "What is Second Life?" for an answer and a link titled "Make Money," which shows you how to profit from playing.
- www.runescape.com: RuneScape also has a good help section, and it's cheaper than some other online fantasy games.
- http://everquest.station.sony.com: Sony's *EverQuest* offers a free trial.

CHAPTER 33

GIVE IT AWAY AND MAKE IT PAY

PROFIT FROM E-BOOKS

A few years back, my e-book on cheap homes was selling slowly, so I tried a new approach. I put the 30 chapters on 30 pages of a web site, added pay-per-click ads to those pages, prepared 30 e-mails, and loaded them into auto-responder, which sends out each message automatically, one per week in this case. On the sales page I added a subscription form for the free version. Subscribers got an e-mail with a link to a chapter each week and could buy the complete e-book if they became impatient. Soon I was making more money from the advertising on those 30 pages than I previously made in book sales. In addition, I was selling more books! Readers liked what they read and wanted the whole book right away.

That's one example of how to make money giving away e-books. I once spent two days writing a 40-page e-book on meditation, which I gave to my *Brainpower Newsletter* subscribers, making hundreds of dollars in the first few weeks. The book had affiliate links in it for my favorite meditation CDs, and I was paid a $42 commission for each sale I referred.

You don't even have to write your own books. In 2001 Vic Johnson started giving away an e-book version of the out-of-copyright book *As a Man Thinketh*, by James Allen, to build a mailing list and promote his web site. Within a few years he had given away 400,000 copies and was making hundreds of thousands of dollars annually from his site, partly by selling self-development products. For more ways to make money doing this, see the resources section for a free chapter from one of my own e-books.

Money

This is a low-risk way to make a lot of money. You can start with nothing but your existing computer and Internet connection, use free tools to make the e-book, and a free blog where you promote and sell it. That doesn't mean it's easy. With practice you can write an e-book in a week, but the best writing in the world doesn't make money without proper marketing, so learn and practice that above all.

I give away e-books, sell them, and use various other strategies. But the revenue from e-book sales and giveaways is a small part of our business, with profits of just $15,000 or so in 2010. Vic Johnson started out in 2001 giving away an e-book and did $671,000 in sales in 2007.

How to Get Started

Get a free PDF converter at Cutepdf.com (much easier to use than Adobe software). Write your book or report with any common word processing program, and then make it into a PDF version, which is the standard for e-books now. Simple online tutorials can show you how to upload an e-book to a blog or web site.

What to write? List several subjects that interest you, choose the one with the most market demand, and start researching and writing.

Resources

- *How to Write and Sell Simple Information for Fun and Profit* by Robert Bly (Linden Publishing, 2010).
- www.freelancewritingsuccess.com/ebooks.php: Information on e-books and other ways to make money writing.
- www.writingforyourwealth.com: There are a couple of posts here on how to make money giving away e-books.
- www.thebulletpoint.com/e-books.html: A free chapter from my e-book *You Can Make Money Writing*.
- www.the-ultralight-site.com/backpacking-book.html: An example of a backpacking e-book I give away (it is one of my best sellers).

CHAPTER 34

AUTOMATIC PROFITS FROM WRITING

AUTO-RESPONDER E-MAIL NEWSLETTERS

How can I produce content for my six different e-mail newsletters weekly? I can't. Only my *Brainpower Newsletter* is put together each week. The rest were set up years ago and are sent out automatically. Subscribe to my *Unusual Ways* newsletter, for example, and every week you'll get an issue with ways to make and save money. There are 70 issues. If I want to add more I can, but if not, I just let the whole thing run on automatic, making money day and night from the ads in the mailings and on the pages to which readers are directed.

E-mail newsletters are available for baseball fans, anarchists, backpackers, dog lovers, and more. If you're passionate about anything, and others share your passion, you can create an online newsletter. You can even make one on a subject you know nothing about, using free content provided by others (they get a link to their web sites in exchange for you using their articles).

Some newsletters should be done fresh every week, like those covering current events. When information is less time sensitive, you can create 52 issues full of great content, load them into an auto-responder, and put the subscription form on your blog or web site. Your work on the newsletter is then done, but with proper marketing the revenue can continue for many years.

Money

Some sell their newsletters, but it's easier to get subscribers with free ones, and many ways are available to monetize them. Every issue of *Unusual Ways* sells my e-books, has links to affiliate products, and links to pages on the web site, which are monetized with pay-per-click ads. It's difficult to say what the revenue would be without it, but UnusualWaystoMakeMoney.com made less than

$2,000 annually before I added the newsletter in 2007 and over $14,000 in 2010. Thousands of visitors who might have come once get sent back to the site every week thanks to the newsletter.

The ultimate potential? Who can say how much credit to give newsletters for the success of some million-dollar web sites, but a common metric is used, which is value per subscriber, either annual or lifetime. I've seen sites claim to make $60 per subscriber per year, but $1 is a more common estimate. I wish I did that with my 34,000 *Brainpower Newsletter* subscribers, but I'm no marketing whiz. On the other hand, subscribers can be sold too. I recently saw a newsletter with over a million subscribers. Based on current prices, he could probably sell the list for a cool $1 million.

How to Get Started

If you already have a web site, you have a subject for your newsletter. Otherwise, enter "free keyword research" in Google to find one of the many tools that show the search traffic for various phrases. Do some research and target a high-traffic niche that you are interested in writing about. Several places host free blogs if you want to start cheaply. You'll need to pay for an e-mail autoresponder. I use AWeber.com. Several companies offer plans starting at less than $20 monthly.

Resources

- *E-Newsletters That Work* by Michael J. Katz (Xlibris, 2003): This book is highly rated by readers, but this is a changing industry so supplement it with more recent information.
- www.healthyhappydogs.com: A dog-health newsletter with 12,000 subscribers.
- http://bestezines.com: An index of thousands of online newsletters; you can add yours to the list here.
- www.themeditationsite.com/newsletter.html: An example of a newsletter that is preprogrammed to send out 43 weekly mailings.

CHAPTER 35

PAID TO WRITE ABOUT FEET

NICHE BLOGS

Hemant Mehta, a Chicago atheist, wrote *I Sold My Soul on eBay* based on an auction in which he promised to attend a church with an open mind—one day for each $10 bid he received. The winning bidder paid $504, making this a weird way to make money, but also a one-time deal. Then Mehta used the experience to create a successful blog called *The Friendly Atheist*. You can see how he monetizes it at FriendlyAtheist.com. Yes, you really can blog about unusual topics and make money.

A blog is like a personal web site where you write about yourself, your opinions, or a subject you're passionate about (all the same thing for some writers). You can find blogs about trees, worms, cars, real estate, and even feet. Of course, some topics hold much more profit potential (stock trading trumps poetry), but some money can be made with almost any niche.

If you like the idea of writing when and how you like, on matters that you care about, and making money doing it, create a blog. And you don't have to stop with one. If you have several interests (who doesn't?), create several blogs. Perhaps all will be fun and one or two will also make money.

Money

My *New Ideas Blog* promotes my site, 999ideas.com, but I rarely add to it now, and it makes only a little extra cash for me. A lesson here might be to concentrate on a few core ventures rather than trying to do e-books, web sites, courses, newsletters, blogs, books, and six other things, as I do. Then again, all these little streams of cash add up to a river. There *is* real money in blogging. Just consider the blog that Steve Pavlina created. Coming from a troubled background, he turned things around and in 2004 started his self-development blog, StevePavlina.com. By 2006 he was making over $1,000—per day! That was without spending any money on marketing or promotion.

How to Get Started

You can start for free at Blogger.com and other hosts, but if you are seriously committed to making money with it, get your own site. A domain name is $10 per year, and hosting is as little as $6 monthly. You can use the free software from WordPress, which is one of the most common blog platforms online now. Its famous five-minute installation should take you only five hours.

Blog daily until you get the hang of it and build up the size of your site. Later you should try to have some fresh content every week or so at a minimum. Most blog platforms allow visitor comments, and this "community building" is a crucial part of success according to some Internet marketers. On the other hand, some of the more successful blogs (including StevePavlina.com) do not allow comments. Spammers will target you if you allow comments, and it can be a lot of work to monitor or individually approve each entry. You might allow them at first and shut them off later if it becomes too much trouble.

Resources

- *Blogging For Dummies,* Third edition, by Susannah Gardner and Shane Birley (Wiley Publishing, 2010).
- www.howtostartablog.org: A short tutorial that covers some of the technical aspects of starting a blog.
- www.footstar.co.uk: An example of a blog . . . about feet.
- www.stevepavlina.com/blog/2006/05/how-to-make-money-from-your-blog: A 7,000-word article detailing how to make blogging pay.
- http://blogcarnival.com: Submit your best posts here to get more traffic.

CHAPTER 36

BE MASTER OF YOUR DOMAINS

INTERNET NAMES BUYER AND SELLER

ARoseByAnyName.com would not smell nearly as sweet as roses.com—at least not to a domain-name investor. Simple names are more valuable. As I write this, RedWine.com just sold for $150,000, and Druid.com sold for $30,000. I'm certain that RedWineForSale .com and TheDruidWebsite.com will never get that much, although they may be worth something. After all, OntarioHomesForSale.com sold for $2,788 this week. The speculative part of this business involves buying good names cheap and selling them for more. For example, you might watch the thousands of name deletions auctioned daily by sites like Snapnames.com or Namejet.com, and win a site like SewerCleaner.com with your $400 bid (it sold for $2,250 this week). You can approach owners of inactive sites with good names and buy from them directly, and cheaply.

Speculating is only one way to invest. You can also buy domain names based on projected traffic and use domain-parking services to make money from visitors. For example, I bought www1040.com (note the lack of a dot) for $300, and collected $10 per month from the clicks on the ads that people found when they went there (I later sold it for a profit). This isn't just about misspelled names and typos. When a site is abandoned, people may try to visit for years, and that traffic makes the domain valuable.

Money

There is big profit potential in speculation, but it's more art than science. Would you buy rentmybooks.com for $500? Excellent decision—it just sold for $2,500. You paid $4,000 for vintageyacht.com? Sorry. It sold for $2,000. Registering unclaimed names of local businesses or almost-memorable ones like WhereToBuySkis.com is safer. Park them with a monetization service, perhaps make half of the annual fee back in revenue, and hope someone offers you $100 or more for some of them . . . someday. A domain-name investor I know has sold names for hundreds of dollars that he registered for under $10. He has sold names for thousands of dollars that he bought at deletion auctions for $60.

Less-speculative investors buy domains based on the projected income. For example, one domain-name investor recently wrote that last year she made $468 from a real estate domain, and $179 from a diet domain, and $269 from another domain. That may not sound like a lot, but what if you invested an average of $100 for each of those and parlayed profits into a thousand more? Average $50 net income per domain, and you make $50,000 annually—and you would be a small player. A few years ago Kevin Ham had 300,000 domains that generated an estimated $70 million annually. Yun Ye sold his portfolio of 100,000 names for $164 million.

How to Get Started

Register a name you like just to get familiar with the process. Attend an auction and buy a name for $100 or less. Visit forums where domain-name investors hang out. Start small and parlay your profits to give yourself time to learn the art of domain-name investing before you invest larger amounts. As soon as you have the minimum required, place your names with a parking service to generate revenue.

Resources

- *Buying and Selling Domain Names 101: How to Buy and Sell Domain Names for Fun and Profits* by Zach Wilson (CreateSpace, 2010).
- http://dnjournal.com: This is *the* place for news about domain sales.
- www.parked.com: Example of a domain-parking service.
- www.websiteproperties.com: Example of a domain-name investor/seller; click "Premium Domain Names."
- www.dnforum.com: A discussion forum for domain-name investors.

CHAPTER 37

WHAT'S YOUR OPINION WORTH?

ONLINE PRODUCT-REVIEWING

The basic idea of an affiliate review web site is to test or investigate products and tell people what you think. You get paid when they click on your affiliate links and buy something. If that sounds interesting, here's some more good news: You can start an affiliate review web site or blog for $100 and run it for less than $30 monthly. This is a very low-risk business.

You have to tell your visitors you're getting paid for sales, but this doesn't mean you can't be honest. After all, if there are six sellers of exercise equipment willing to pay a commission for referred sales, at least a couple of them are doing something right—tell your readers which ones. If you review e-books, some of them have to be good, so point your readers in the right direction and collect a commission for each sale. By the way, more than 10,000 e-books and other digital products are sold on ClickBank.com, and they pay up to 70 percent of the price as a commission.

Money

Can you make $100,000 your first year in affiliate marketing, as the sales pitches claim? Probably not easily, but success stories abound. Fergal Downes, a martial arts fighter and former telemarketer who now runs WealthyAffiliate-Reviewer .com, started selling affiliate products in 2008, and he was making $100 per day within a few months. Chris Rempel, the creator of TheLazyMarketer.com and master of the review-site strategy, made $100,000 in his first six months.

My own results have been less dramatic (our pay-per-click ads do far better), but I do enjoy the $1,000 or so in monthly commissions that we get from the few affiliate products we promote. And I like the fact that my meditation CD review site now requires only a few hours annually to maintain the income stream it produces. Residual income is a wonderful thing. Do the work up front, and even if you grow to just $2,000 monthly from your review sites, that income can keep coming in for years without much additional effort.

With small markets you might have to build many review web sites targeting different niches. It may be difficult to generate more than $600 monthly reviewing hats (yes, some hat sellers do offer affiliate commissions), but a dozen sites each generating $600 per month create an income stream of $86,000 annually.

How to Get Started

Choose the products to review, then get an appropriately named web site or blog. Although thousands of get-rich products have affiliate programs, it's better to start in smaller niches that have less competition. Online affiliate programs are offered by cement companies, pet care businesses, backpacking equipment suppliers . . . the list goes on. Avoid small-commission products. Reviewing paper books and sending traffic to an online bookseller, for example, will net you as little as 40 cents per sale. You won't sell enough books to make it worthwhile. I like to see at least $10 for an e-book sale I refer, and with meditation programs I get up to $42.

Resources

- *Make a Fortune Promoting Other People's Stuff Online: How Affiliate Marketing Can Make You Rich* by Rosalind Gardner (McGraw-Hill, 2007).
- www.bestmeditationcds.com: My own review site for meditation CDs.
- www.thebulletpoint.com/review-site.html: Links to everything necessary to start an affiliate review web site.
- http://lifetimecommissions.com/directories.html: A directory of lifetime commission affiliate programs; refer a customer and if they're still buying products 10 years later, you still get a percentage.

PART FIVE

GREEN JOBS AND BUSINESSES

The his section might be my weak point from the perspective of personal experience, although as a landscaper I never used chemicals, and collecting discarded cans and bottles for their returnable deposits not only directly cleaned up the environment but also helped recycle metals, glass, and plastics. I certainly understand the appeal of green jobs and businesses. They can help us create or maintain a better world to live in—and there might be some real money in them as well.

From selling biodegradable caskets to salvaging and recycling valuable platinum from catalytic converters in junkyards, this section covers some of the less common ways to make money in green industries. Are there decent income and profit opportunities here? You bet there are. And it is a safe prediction that there will be growth in electronic waste recycling, providing specialty organic foods, and many other green industries.

DAVE HARTKOP, SOLAR ROAST COFFEE

Dave Hartkop and his brother Michael roast their coffee beans using only the concentrated power of the sun, having made their first roaster from an old satellite dish in 2004. Today they have two coffee shops and they ship their products all over the country from their headquarters in Pueblo, Colorado. I asked Dave about their motivations and what it took to make a profit.

What did you and Michael do before starting Solar Roast Coffee?

Michael went to college for business at the University of Launceston in Tasmania. Then he worked a couple different coffee shops . . . he did a coffee-roasting apprenticeship. I got a degree in film production and communications from Loyola Marymount in Los Angeles. I worked freelance doing digital special effects for TV commercials and music videos for five or six years before becoming obsessed with solar energy and getting sick of living in LA.

I understand you use organic coffee beans, and solar roasting is more environmentally friendly than other methods. Were environmental factors part of your motivation for getting into this particular niche?

It has been part of the total picture in terms of what we want to present: organic and environmentally friendly roasting. When we started, we were not organically certified but were able to still say that we were the most ecologically friendly roasters in the world, despite our being so small.

I can confirm that your coffee is absolutely delicious, but has flavor consistency been a challenge with this method of roasting?

These are all-manual machines. . . . The consistency you taste is all my brother Michael's doing! (Occasionally, he burns a batch, and we label it with a gritty atomic-blast pic and ship it to family back east under the name "scorched earth!") It's too burnt to sell, but our uncle in Michigan loves it.

How long was it before you were making a profit?

Profit? What's that?? Actually, I'm proud to say we've been "in the green" for going on a year. It seriously took us two years of business in Pueblo before we could say that! (If we'd known what we were doing, and not purchased a bunch of nonworking junk along with our first coffeehouse, it would have been less time. Take time to try everything! Also, pay an inspector! Geez . . .)

Do you make most of your profits from coffee, or are sales of other drinks and foods a bigger part of the business now that you have two retail locations?

We really do make most of our money one cup at a time. Wholesale on-line is the easiest, but with the lowest profit margin. Personally, I like the bulk wholesale route because it is a lot less trouble to just produce and ship, but coffeehouses are excellent exposure and wonderful places to hang out and meet people!

Do you sell your coffee directly to other coffee shops around the country, or do you have a distributor?

Early on, we tried to go with a few different distributors, but they were either ineffective or too expensive. All of our current customers are accounts that the two of us went out and got ourselves. . . . Nothing sells itself! We are in touch with a larger-scale distributor, with whom we plan to distribute . . . when we're to that point.

What advice can you offer those who might want to get into a specialty food or drink business?

Well, if you have something that you believe people will want to buy from you, then go for it! It takes time to get any kind of wholesale going, so direct retail may be the best way to start off. And don't get discouraged when it takes a long time *to get sales rolling. First of all, nobody* ever *calls you back. . . . An in-person sales call is much more effective. You have to visit once, follow up in person a second time, and then make about four or five follow-up calls over the following one to two months to get someone to sign up. Start a spreadsheet with names, numbers, and logs of your contacts! And then* use *it!*

Also, it's important to really focus on your core business. We've been roasting and selling solar-roasted coffee since 2004, and that's what we do!

CHAPTER 38

GREEN DEATH

ENVIRONMENTALLY FRIENDLY FUNERALS

More than ever, people want to be environmentally conscious up to—and beyond—the end. In the funeral and burial industry, that means no embalming fluids, no concrete burial vaults, and biodegradable caskets as well as other earth-friendly options. Natural burials without any casket are also becoming more common where the laws permit them. Green cemeteries, which allow for these kinds of burials, are flourishing. In England, for example, the first one opened in 1993, and now there are more than 200 of them. Expect the United States to catch up soon.

The more the public is educated about these options, the more common it will become for people to arrange for environmentally friendly funerals and natural burials. In addition to providing biodegradable clothing and caskets, green funeral homes arrange for funerals that use only organic flowers grown locally, catering using organic food, and almost anything a client might like. Cremation is also considered a part of this general trend. It may not be as green as a natural burial in one's favorite blanket, but it is still much more earth friendly than traditional funerals and burials.

Money

How much do employees of funeral homes make? Among other factors, it depends on the position. Funeral directors average $60,390 annually in the United States. Funeral attendants average only $23,880. Current online job postings offer base-plus-commission pay of $55,000 to $70,000 annually for sales positions, assuming sales targets are hit.

If more money is your goal, employment provides the training and experience needed to someday start your own business. Revenue sources in this market include funeral and cremation services, the sale of natural wood caskets, other burial materials, organic flowers, organic catering, and bio-degradable burial urns. The big profit potential in the future is in making more people aware of green options so they can preplan for these. Possibilities outside funeral homes include making and selling green caskets and related products.

In researching this I found more than a hundred funeral homes with an estimated annual revenue of $5 million or more. Most of these aren't seriously competing in the green part of the market. With high profit margins in the industry in general, and low competition in this particular area, you can see that catering to people's needs in the green funeral and green burial niches offers some real profit potential.

How to Get Started

Funeral directors, also called morticians and undertakers, are licensed in all states and usually have at least a two-year degree in mortuary science. For sales positions, on-the-job training is common. Requirements vary, in part depending on whether you sell burial insurance or just help clients preplan funerals. Starting as a funeral attendant is an easier way to get hired. You'll do things like arrange flowers and lights, move caskets, and escort mourners to their seats.

To move into the green funeral niche, learn about the market and products. A bit of research can make you more knowledgeable than most funeral home employees. You can potentially open up or expand the green market for a funeral home, and you might present yourself in that way when you apply for a job or for a promotion.

Resources

- www.funeraljobs.com: Information on the industry and job listings.
- www.greenburialcouncil.org: An eco-certification program and lists of approved burial grounds, funeral providers, cemeteries, cremation disposition programs, and products.
- www.nfda.org: National Funeral Directors Association; a good place to start educating yourself. For a job search, click "Find a Funeral Home" on the home page to locate those closest to you.
- www.greenburials.org: Information and a short list of green cemeteries.

CHAPTER 39

SLEEP ON THIS IDEA

RECYCLING MATTRESSES

There was a time when I bought used mattresses to save money. You can still find them for sale at thrift stores, used furniture stores, and from individuals. My wife and I wouldn't consider buying a used mattress now, and many people feel the same way. In fact, with increasing sensitivity to hygiene issues, and with the spread of bedbugs in recent years, the direct selling of used bedding is less common. Most mattresses are discarded when replaced now, but the garbage man won't take them, and it's no fun hauling them to the dump on the roof of the car. That's where the recycling businesses come into the picture.

Still a relatively new field, so far only a handful of mattress-recycling companies exist, but you can expect that to change. More than 10 million mattresses are thrown out every year in the United States. If you start a business in this niche, you'll get paid for drop-offs, and to pick up old mattresses, and then you'll do one of two things. First, you'll re-cover and/or rebuild salvageable mattresses. For example, MBC Mattress Co. in Corona, California, receives hundreds of old mattresses daily, bakes them at 205 degrees for 90 minutes to kill bedbugs and germs, then replaces the foam and other components as necessary and sells the rebuilt mattresses to retailers, colleges (for dorm rooms), and hotels. Second, you'll take apart the worst mattresses and sell or otherwise recycle the components. The foam is used for making insulation and carpet padding, for example. Some companies claim up to 90 percent efficiency in recycling all the materials.

Money

If there are other recyclers in the area, you compete on the basis of their prices for accepting or picking up old mattresses. If not, you compete against the cost and trouble the customer faces taking the bedding to the dump. Conigliaro

Industries, near Boston, charges $8 to $18 to accept a mattress. Bed Busters, operating in the San Francisco area, will not take drop-offs and charges $48 for a twin and $88 to pick up a king-size mattress. This upfront money covers much of your costs, and then you make your profit selling the reconditioned mattresses or their components.

MBC sells rebuilt ones for about $200. Other companies typically sell reconditioned mattresses for $50 to $150. One entrepreneur in southern California gets about 25 mattresses for free each week and wholesales them to a distributor who takes them to Mexico to sell. Competition is still light in this industry. I found data on only five mattress-recycling companies, but two of those do more than $500,000 in annual revenue.

How to Get Started

You can get into this green business in several ways. One is to work as an employee for one of the mattress recyclers out there. In addition to the ones listed in the resources section, you can search "mattress recycling" at Manta. com to see if any companies are near you. They list the address and usually the phone number of the companies. Employment can teach you what you need to start your own business.

To start small in this field, you can advertise locally to pick up mattresses for a small fee, then either find a wholesale buyer or recondition them in your garage for resale, and expand from there.

Resources

- http://bedbusters.com: An example of a company that recycles mattresses.
- www.ninelivesmattressrecycling.com: Another example.
- www.themattresslady.com/recycling_mattresses_001181.html: Information on recycling mattresses.
- www.ohiomattressrecovery.com: A video of the mattress-recycling process.

CHAPTER 40

COMPUTER GARBAGE MAN

ELECTRONIC-WASTE RECYCLING

More than 60 million computers are traded in or thrown away every year in the United States. In fact, only 15 percent of electronic devices are recycled, according to the Environmental Protection Agency. When discarded in landfills, computers and other electronics release toxic materials, including lead, mercury, and cadmium, into the soil, groundwater, and air. Proper disposal means taking those electronics to a recycler, but in many areas there are not many around. That spells opportunity for those who want a green business *and* big potential.

With computer recycling, you usually charge for each item dropped off. (In our small town, even the thrift stores charge $7 to take an old computer or monitor.) Then you do one of two things with each computer. You rebuild it to sell, or you disassemble it and sell the valuable components before sending the rest to the dump. If you like building things and tearing them apart, this could be a fun and profitable venture.

Money

A typical consumer recycling charge for a computer is $5. The charge to drop off a monitor is as high as $15 because there are fewer recoverable materials. For printers, typewriters, fax machines, scanners, and copiers, you can charge $5 to $15 each. Some companies charge extra to destroy hard drives.

After being paid recycling fees, you make money from selling computers that you rebuild, or from selling the scrap components from any of the electronics you accept. Reconditioned computers typically sell for $100 to $250. For those that can't be rebuilt, and for other electronics, salable salvage items include copper wires, circuit boards (there is gold and silver in these), metal casings, plastics, and usable parts like hard drives (after clearing the data) and keyboards. What is the potential for this business? Recent data shows that at least several dozen computer-recycling companies have annual revenues of more than $1 million.

How to Get Started

If you haven't ever built or rebuilt a computer, you might want to start with any old one you have around. You might also look up the nearest computer-recycling business and see if they are hiring. On-the-job training is common, and a few weeks or months of employment will teach you what you need to know and tell you if you like the work.

You can start your business at home if necessary. Recycling of components can be done in a garage or basement until you need a larger space. See how long it takes to tear apart and sort the parts, and get quotes from buyers for the salvaged materials. At some point determine the gross revenue per computer, which will tell you how fast a teardown needs to be to afford employees. Advertising will be necessary, but you should also call schools, businesses, and other who might have closets or rooms full of old computers they need to get rid of. Getting large quantities of computers at a time is more efficient, even if you have to pick them up for a small fee. If you're not proficient at rebuilding computers, learn to determine which can be saved, and wholesale those to someone who can make them ready to retail.

Resources

- www.recyclingsecrets.com/starting-electronics-recycling.htm: Tips for starting a computer-recycling business.
- http://en.wikipedia.org/wiki/Computer_recycling: A good overview of the reasons for and process of recycling computers.
- www.thegreenpc.com: An example of a large computer-recycling operation.
- www.youtube.com: Search "rebuild computer" to find several good video tutorials.
- www.webuyics.com: A buyer of circuit boards and other electronics scrap.

CHAPTER 41

BE AN OIL-TANK TYCOON

OLD FUEL-TANK REMOVER

When oil tanks leak, they usually need to be replaced, and regulations are getting tougher all the time. This is why testing and removing them, along with the associated environmental remediation work, is a growth industry. Both underground and aboveground tanks are prone to corrosion and need inspection. Removal, if necessary, is not something that homeowners can easily do on their own, and few try. Permits are required, specific procedures are mandated by state and federal regulations, and usually heavy equipment is involved. Oil and sludge needs to be suctioned out using special tools. A good tank-removal company has the right equipment, knows the local codes, gets the permit for the homeowner, and reports the removal and remediation work done to the appropriate authorities as required.

This is a capital-intensive business compared to most in this book, but you can receive good pay as an employee, making that the sensible way to start. You get to work outdoors while helping homeowners avoid liability and helping to keep the environment clean.

Money

Oil-tank-removal employees are called "environmental engineering technicians" in Labor Department statistics, and workers in this classification average $45,700 annually, with 10 percent of them making more than $70,800. The top-paying states for this position have average annual wages of about $55,000 to $61,000, and are Washington, California, South Carolina, Alaska, and Nevada.

The prices for tank removal are based in part on the size of the tank and the difficulty of accessing it. Guidelines posted online by companies suggest (although each case can be unique) that smaller tanks typically cost $1,300 to remove, while larger ones can go as high as $4,000. For example, a Brewster, New York, company estimates that to remove a buried 550-gallon tank *and* install a 275-gallon aboveground tank costs $3,200. It typically takes a day or less to do a job like that, if there are no complications, and no additional remediation work related to leaks.

It is difficult to imagine how you would start a business of this type with no experience. It is heavily regulated and requires expensive equipment. Although difficult to confirm, it is a good guess that most owners of these businesses first worked in the field as employees—that's how you get the experience. And what is the potential if you go from employee to building your own company? Of the hundreds of environmental remediation companies that do oil-tank removal as their primary service, about 90 have annual revenues of $5 million or more.

How to Get Started

Employment requirements vary quite a bit. Some companies want a bachelor's degree for you to be a technician, even if the degree is in an unrelated area. Others will start you out as an "environmental remediation laborer," which pays less and has fewer requirements. All companies will want you to get one or more certifications, although some current job listings state that you only need to obtain these within six months of being hired. The most common one is the 40-hour HAZWOPER (Hazardous Waste Operations and Emergency Response) certification. Other OSHA certifications might be required.

Resources

- www.commtank.com: An example of a company in the business of removing oil tanks.
- www.inspectapedia.com/oiltanks/tanks.htm: Dozens of pages of information on oil tanks and removing them.
- www.envirotechservicesinc.com: Another example of an oil-tank testing and removal company.
- www.natlenvtrainers.com: Offers HAZWOPER training and certification.

CHAPTER 42

CASH FROM CATALYTIC CONVERTERS

SCRAP METALS SALVAGER AND SELLER

Flooded parking lots were in the news in Colorado Springs last night, after criminals cut fittings off sprinkler systems, to sell the brass for $1.50 per pound. In Detroit, families return from vacation to find their homes' aluminum siding removed, destined to pay for someone's next drug fix. When platinum topped $2,000 per ounce in 2008, Wired.com reported on thieves crawling under cars and removing catalytic converters to sell for as much as $200. These are stories from the dark side of high metal prices. Fortunately, legal ways are available to make money in scrap metals.

A while ago I cleaned our garage and gave various metal items to a neighbor. He added them to the neat piles behind his house, which he cashes in every few months. It's just extra income for him, but you can make big money with metals. The ones commonly recycled include brass, copper, aluminum, silver, and platinum. Making money with them can be like a treasure hunt. I saw a set of aluminum car wheels at a rummage sale the other day, and now, having done the research, I know I was looking at a $20 profit there. Scavenging at rummage sales is small time, to be sure, but it's a fun way to start.

Money

Catalytic converters provide the most money in the smallest item for most metals recyclers. Some process the platinum and other metals (they may have palladium and rhodium) themselves, but this is tricky, time consuming, and possibly dangerous, so you're better off selling the whole unit or the core. With an average of about three grams of platinum in each, catalytic converters currently sell for between $50 and $125.

101

Copper currently sells for about $2.30 per pound, and you can sometimes find it in large quantities. Buildings scheduled for demolition may have copper tubing throughout. Both automobiles and air conditioners have up to 50 pounds of copper in them. A single junk car might have aluminum wheels worth $40, copper in the radiator and other parts worth $100, platinum in the catalytic converter worth $150, and other metals. Computers have recoverable gold, platinum, silver, copper, palladium, and aluminum. You usually just sell the circuit boards to computer scrap processors.

The profit potential in recycling metals is enormous if you eventually scale up your business. Stephen Greer (see the resources section) bought a one-way ticket to Hong Kong just out of college and, stumbling into the industry without intention, built a $250 million scrap metal business. According to recent data, hundreds of scrap metal companies in the United States do $10 million or more in annual revenue.

How to Get Started

Call scrap dealers to see what they buy and to get current prices. Take notes. You can start out using a bathroom scale for larger items and perhaps a kitchen scale for smaller ones, like silver utensils. Initially you can try rummage sales and ask people about any items you see in their yards. Talk to owners of abandoned homes about removing copper pipes and other metals, perhaps for a share of the revenue. You can work from home until you find larger opportunities that require more space, like when you start buying and stripping junk cars.

Resources

- *Starting from Scrap: An Entrepreneurial Success Story* by Stephen Greer (Burford Books, 2010).
- www.catalyticconverterscrap.com: An auction site for scrap catalytic converters.
- www.recycleinme.com: A place to buy and sell scrap metals and learn more about the business.

CHAPTER 43

SOLAR-ROASTED COFFEE

UNIQUE GREEN FOODS AND DRINKS SELLER

When we are in Pueblo, Colorado, we sometimes stop at Solar Roast Coffee for a cup of delicious java. Its beans are roasted in special ovens that use the concentrated heat of the sun (see the interview with Dave Hartkop). This is a good example of what's possible with environmentally friendly food businesses, which include organic juice bars, vegetarian and vegan restaurants, and eco-cafes. Other niches in green foods involve supplying those cafes and restaurants with new items.

If the green foods industry appeals to you, then your first decision is whether to work with the public directly or to be the one creating and/or delivering the goodies to the retail establishments. Businesses of the latter type can be just as profitable as running a cafe or restaurant and may be easier to start. Before opening their coffeehouses, for example, the owners of Solar Roast Coffee sold to existing ones, and they roasted the first batch of beans in a converted satellite dish in their backyard.

Money

Counter attendants, a category that includes running the register in a coffee shop, average just $18,180 annually, and only about 10 percent of them make over $24,000. The money in selling unique green foods is not in being an employee.

Restaurants and coffeehouses are notoriously risky businesses, whether they're traditional or target the market for green products. But at least 100 coffeehouses in the United States do more than $1 million in annual sales, and profit margins of 25 percent are common, which indicates an average income of about $250,000 for owners of these more successful places. Most are traditional coffee shops and cafes, but green businesses often face less competition and so can be more likely to succeed.

103

Perhaps the more interesting niches are in the creation and distribution of new products that are environmentally friendly. You might make organic cookies that use fruits nobody else is using. Or you can just sell products made by others. For example, more than a hundred companies exist that sell organic wine, and a dozen of those do more than $1 million in annual sales. Most of them are wineries as well, but a distributor who helps market the production from smaller vineyards can do well.

How to Get Started

Employment opportunities in this area are poor (at least the income is), but it still makes sense to work in a restaurant or organic café before trying to start your own. The experience will teach you what's necessary and perhaps give you ideas about what can be done differently for greater success.

If you want to create your own products to sell, you can do this at home until your testing and market research are done. After that, you'll need a commercial kitchen, both to comply with health and safety regulations and to be able to ramp up production. To keep costs low, lease an existing kitchen. Bakers, for example, often use their equipment only during the night and early morning hours and will rent out the facilities during the day.

Resources

- *The Green Foods Bible: Everything You Need to Know about Barley Grass, Wheatgrass, Kamut, Chlorella, Spirulina and More* by David Sandoval (Freedom Publishing Company, 2007).
- www.namastejuicebar.com: An example of an organic juice bar.
- www.frugalmarketing.com/dtb/cool-cafe.shtml: An article on how to run a frugal cafe and make it a popular hangout.
- www.solarroast.com: The web site of Solar Roast Coffee.

PART SIX

HOME-BASED MONEY MAKERS

I always loved the idea of making money from home, especially after I married Ana. For years friends came to my house to borrow money, and I was happy to hold a television or jewelry as collateral for the 10 percent-monthly-interest loans. I had roommates and even rented out a shed as a bedroom after running a buried extension cord to it for power. I operated a closet grocery store for my tenants. When I married, my wife didn't like having people live with us, but fortunately we discovered Internet marketing, writing, and publishing—all great ways to stay home and make a living.

The home-based money makers in this section are of two types. The first type is jobs and businesses that almost never require you to leave the house. All of the Internet opportunities covered earlier could be included in this, but those deserved their own section. The other type is ways to make money that allow you to use your home as your base but that will require you to go out into the world as well. Either type has real advantages, including more time with family, a 30-second morning commute, and working in your pajamas— at least part of the day.

MARK SHAPIRO, JUDGMENT BROKER

Mark Shapiro, the founder of the web site JudgmentBuy.com refers to himself as both a *judgment catalyst* and a *judgment broker*. His web site brings judgment enforcers together to trade information and ideas and provides a place for those who have an uncollected judgment to find a recovery professional. I asked him about what it takes to get into and succeed in this business.

105

I understand that the laws are different in each state, but in general, can anyone become a judgment enforcer?

Anyone with reasonably good health, with the ability to learn and work hard, and go for a time without income, can become a judgment enforcer. The JE business requires one to dig in and study and work for a long time to learn the business. It also requires one to continue learning the business after they are established, for as long as they are in the business. Judgment enforcement is usually hard work, requiring a lot of patience, the ability to do legal research, along with the ability to go periods of time with no income. This means someone in your family will need to have an income coming in, until you get well established.

Does a person need to invest much to become a judgment enforcer?

Probably $1,000 for training courses, phones, fax, data service subscriptions, a locking file cabinet. Best to have a web site, a separate phone, and fax line.

Can a JE buy judgments as a way to make more money than through enforcement for others?

Actually to enforce judgments for others one must buy all judgments outright. Most judgment enforcers buy them on a future-pay basis, keeping 50 percent or so of what they recover from the debtor and passing the rest on to the original judgment creditor. In some states, and some situations, judgment enforcers pay 1 percent to 10 percent cash up front for the judgment, and then enforce the judgment and keep any profits for themselves.

Will a beginning JE generally make more money doing the work himself or referring business to others for a commission?

The best solution is to do both. A judgment enforcer should work judgments local to them, and refer ones too far away to a judgment broker to earn a referral fee. A good judgment enforcer never works judgments they can't handle. When starting out, don't work fraudulent transfer judgments, or judgments where the debtor is more than a half hour's drive away. Pass along or refer such judgments to a broker or a more qualified judgment enforcer.

What are some of the things a person needs to learn to become a judgment enforcer?

The laws of their state, and at least one judgment-recovery training course.

Where can a person learn what he needs to know?

The Internet: http://forum.judgmentbuy.com is a good start. There is a review of training courses there. I also recommend the National Judgment Network.

What are a few of the ways a JE finds business?

One must find judgment leads. These can be found at courthouses, advertising, or buying judgment leads.

What is a reasonable income goal if a person learns what is necessary, pursues the easiest large judgments possible, and works hard?

Judgment enforcers have similar success rates as musicians. In both fields, a lot of people dabble. Relatively few study, work enough, for long enough, to make good money. In the first year, I would guess most part-time judgment enforcers earn less than $4,000. Those that keep working earn more and more every year. The right person, in the right place, can be earning $50,000 to $300,000 a year, but that is based on luck, skill, and how hard one works.

CHAPTER 44

BE A HOME-BASED SLUMLORD

ROOM RENTER TO FRIENDS

My first house was a mobile home on a small lot that I bought for $19,500. I rented out rooms to friends and coworkers, and a few strangers from time to time. In a few years the mortgage was paid off. I built a small efficiency apartment on the back side and rented all three rooms, taking in $65, $75, and $85 weekly for the three original bedrooms, with all utilities included. That adds up to more than $11,000 annually. Here's some more math: The total expenses for utilities, property taxes, insurance, repairs—everything—averaged just under $300 per month, or $3,600 per year. I lived for free and had over $7,000 of extra income.

If that sounds interesting, it gets better. Today, in many parts of the country you can rent a bedroom in your home for $125 or more weekly. Just two rooms rented out would mean $13,000 in your pocket every year, minus the minimal expense of having a couple of extra people using water and lights. In many areas, if you rent rooms in your own home by the week, you are more of a hotel operator than a landlord. This gray area of the law means evictions are easier and regulations looser, especially if you don't bother with security deposits (I never did).

Money

If you rent rooms only in your own home, this is just a nice extra income. You can increase revenue by adding bedrooms to the house or by adding a small apartment for you and your family so you can rent all existing space. Clearly this works better with houses that have many bedrooms and in cities where rental demand is strong. If it costs $800 monthly plus utilities for a small apartment in your area, plenty of individuals will want one of your spaces for $150 weekly with everything included. Four such rooms would generate $31,200 annually before vacancies and expenses.

109

To make more money, you can buy houses specifically for the purpose of renting to several individuals. This strategy has made some investors wealthy in college towns where rents are high. In that case you choose your investments according to the number of rooms as much as the location. A big house with five bedrooms and a basement that can be converted into three more can be a real cash cow. By the time you own two or three of these, you have a retirement plan.

How to Get Started

If you are renting out rooms in your own home, think carefully about whether you want to maximize profits by keeping rents high and rooms full, or if you want only friends and people you know renting from you. Have clearly laid-out house rules posted somewhere obvious, and designate space in the refrigerator for each tenant. It is almost always better to charge weekly or per paycheck, and include all utilities in the rent, to simplify things and because this rental market is partly made of people who can't budget well for expenses. Research the going rates for rooms. Finally, see if there are local regulations about unrelated people occupying a house (in some communities it's okay to have six noisy kids and cousins in your house, but not three quiet strangers).

Resources

- *Retire on the House: Using Real Estate to Secure Your Retirement* by Gillette Edmunds (John Wiley & Sons, Inc., 2005): Covers many ways to use your home for extra income, including renting rooms.
- www.99reports.com/boarding-house.html: My own e-book on renting rooms in your home.
- www.easyroommate.com: A great site for finding tenants.

CHAPTER 45

DRIVING HOME YOUR PROFITS

USED CAR SELLER FROM YOUR YARD

Many years ago, a coworker at the casino where I worked asked me to invest in an old fiberglass-body car. He could get it for $2,300 he told me, and sell it for a profit. I had no idea why people would want a 1976 car with transmission problems. He showed me a car guide and convinced me. He bought it for $2,200. I had $3,200 total into it by the time it was repaired, cleaned, and sold two weeks later for $4,200. We made $500 each on that '76 Corvette Stingray. I never knew anything about cars, but I did invest in them with friends several times after that and never lost money.

I know a used car dealer who made a living operating out of his yard. Another man, a neighbor from years ago in northern Michigan, told me he made profits of $30,000 in good years from cars he bought and sold—and he didn't speak much English. He was something of a mechanic, but that is not important for making money with used cars. The key is carefully buying cars for substantially less than they can be sold for. Do that and it's hard to go wrong.

You can do this from your own yard or driveway on a small scale to start. Most states allow you to buy and sell a certain number of cars annually without a dealer license. The risk is low if you start with one car and put the profits into the next one. If you like your results, scale up. You can make big money here.

Money

Start with the low end of the market, where cars sell quickly and risk is low. Search newspaper and online classifieds for cars worth $2,000, and offer $1,000 until you get one. Clean it up, sell it, and repeat the process. Then buy a car for $5,000 that can be retailed for $7,000 or $8,000. You can flip a few cars annually as personal vehicles and a few more in your spouse's name if necessary, but you'll eventually need a dealer's license, which makes doing more deals legal and gets you into dealer-only auctions, where you can find some great deals.

What's the potential if you scale up and start your own car lot? I just searched "used car dealers" at a business-data site, and to narrow the results down to several thousand companies I had to make the revenue criteria $20 million or more annually.

How to Get Started

It is all about buying right, so you need to learn values. Buy a used car price guide or use the free ones online (see the resources section). Assume you'll sell for the average "private party price" at most, not the "dealer price." Customers pay much more when buying from established dealer lots. To be safe, buy for at least $1,000 below what you can sell the car for in front of your house or in the grocery store parking lot. If you need help, partner (in some uncomplicated way) with a friend who knows cars.

Resources

- *Velocity: From the Front Line to the Bottom Line* by Dale Pollak (New Year Publishing, 2010): A guide for when you're ready to grow your used car business.
- www.kbb.com/used-cars: Kelley Blue Book online, with searchable price data for most used cars.
- www.buy-and-sell-cars-for-profit.com: An e-book package on buying and selling used cars.
- www.carbuyingtips.com/sellused.htm: Tips for selling a used car.

CHAPTER 46

MAKING PEOPLE PAY

JUDGMENT ENFORCER

What happens when a landlord gets a court judgment for $4,000 against a tenant who skipped town, or when a roofer gets a $5,000 judgment for back wages a contractor owes him? As often as not, nothing happens. Collection is tough, and until that happens, a judgment is just a piece of paper. This is why there are judgment enforcers, also known as judgment-recovery professionals.

The laws vary, but you do not need to be an attorney in most states to enforce judgments. In some you have to register as a collection agency, but many do not require even that. And what does the work involve? You'll find clients by doing research at courthouses, through advertising, or even by buying judgment leads. Then you'll buy judgments from the holders on the basis of a future payment of 30 to 70 percent of the amount—when it is collected. Once you have a contract, you find the debtors, locate assets they own, and go to courts to get the legal authority to seize those assets. It is an interesting and potentially enjoyable process—if you like investigative work.

Money

You might make a decent income collecting many small judgments, but those who work in this field suggest that the larger ones are more profitable. Collecting 30 percent of a $100,000 judgment is a lot more than 50 percent of a $4,000 one. The larger judgments usually take more time and expense, though, so balance the nature of the judgments against the amount to be collected to maximize profits. Ideally, you want the easiest large judgments you can get.

In addition to buying on the basis of future payment, you can also pay up front. Since you generally pay 10 percent or less of the judgment amount, this can be more profitable if you're good at picking the right ones and are good at your job. It is also riskier: You either lose all of your investment or keep all the money collected. Most judgment enforcers start part-time and make no more than a few thousand dollars their first year. With experience you can make more than $100,000 annually, and a few companies make over $500,000 in annual revenue.

How to Get Started

You can start part time in this industry and wait until you have experience before becoming a full-time professional. Books and free online resources can help, but you may want to pay for a good training course. Start-up costs can be as little as a few hundred dollars. You need patience and a willingness to do a lot of tedious research. You need to not only learn the basics but also have a fair amount of experience to be able to determine which judgments are worth pursuing.

You have another, perhaps easier way to get into the business. It is to concentrate on the research part to find the judgment debts, and then refer these to professionals in the field for a commission. Also, a few of the larger judgment collection companies do hire employees—a low-risk way to gain the experience needed to go it alone.

Resources

- www.judgmentbuy.com: A good overview of the industry, with articles on everything from collection strategies to flipping judgments.
- www.nationaljudgment.net: Learn from professionals and get certified—not a legal requirement, but it gives you credibility.
- www.recoverycourse.com: A course put together by a woman who has worked in the industry for more than 17 years.
- www.judgmentbuyers.com: An example of a judgment-recovery company.

CHAPTER 47

BIG MONEY IN METAL HOUSES

MOBILE HOMES FLIPPER

The first house I owned was a mobile home. I purchased another on a lot nearby, for $19,000 cash, and sold it months later for $22,000, with a down payment of $1,000, to an investor who had dozens of mobile home rentals. I collected 9 percent interest on the balance for many years. I've bought and sold only a few mobile homes—buying my first for $19,500 and selling it for $45,000—but there are investors who specialize in this market, and some of them make a lot of money. If you are interested in great returns on your investments, don't overlook this niche.

It might surprise you to learn that the returns can be even better with mobile homes that do not come with land. Mobile homes on rented lots in parks provide the easiest and lowest-risk way to make high investment returns, even though they go down in value over time while mobiles on land go up. Just buy them cheap from owners who need to sell fast, and sell them for a much higher price by making it easy for the new owner. You help people do better than they would as tenants (unlike when they rent, they own something when they finish paying you), and you make great profits.

Money

With mobile homes in parks, you need to buy low and sell high quickly, which you can do by making it easy for the new buyer. In a typical deal, you find a seller who needs to move, with a home worth $8,000 when cleaned up. He's in a hurry, the home is dirty, and you offer cash today, so he sells it for $5,000. Sales tax, closing costs, cleaning, and a month of lot rent cost you $1,000, so you have $6,000 invested. You target buyers who have little money down and little ability to borrow and sell it for $11,000, with just $1,000 down and payments of $300 monthly at 12 percent interest on the balance of $10,000. For the buyer, the payment and lot rent are usually cheaper than renting an apartment. In less than four years you collect a total of over $13,300 between the down payment and monthly payments—on a $6,000 investment. Investor Lonnie Scruggs once took in $23,747 on a mobile home he first bought for $4,000, by buying it back and reselling it several times.

Although not necessarily using this method, hundreds of companies are selling used mobile homes and making more than $10 million annually, according to recent business data.

How to Get Started

Get familiar with the prices for used mobile homes in your area, using online resources and by talking to dealers and real estate agents who sell mobile homes. Check with the various parks to see what their rules are about investment buyers. They have the right to say if the home stays, and most of the value is lost if you have to move a mobile. Start at the low end to be safe, and parlay your profits into bigger deals.

Resources

- *Mobile Home Wealth: How to Make Money Buying, Selling and Renting Mobile Homes* by Zalman Velvel (Square One Publishers, 2008).
- www.lonniescruggs.net: Lonnie Scruggs is *the* expert on making money with mobile homes; click on "articles" to start your education.
- www.housesunderfiftythousand.com/selling-mobile-homes.html: Tips for getting the most when selling a mobile home.
- www.realtor.com: Mobile homes are sold by many real estate agents, even when in parks, and you can find them listed here.

CHAPTER 48

JUDGING A BOOK BY ITS COVER

USED BOOK SELLER FROM HOME

It is easier than ever to make money selling used books. Gone are the days when you needed to invest thousands of dollars in inventory and thousands more to lease a good retail location. Now you can start with one book, and sell from home. Take some books off your shelf right now and look up the titles on Amazon.com. Under the shopping cart area, click a button that says "Sell yours here." You'll be walked through the process. Once you have a sale, ship the book out by fourth class or "book rate." If that was fun, you might be ready to make a business of this.

That is just one way to make money with used books. You can also set up a web site to sell a certain type, like just cookbooks or only novels. You can wholesale books in larger quantities to other dealers. One successful used bookseller specializes in rare books, which he auctions on eBay. Another started off selling books from his own shelves and now sells 40 to 50 books daily while still working a full-time job.

Money

You need to buy cheap and know which books will sell for how much. Price information is easily available. You can see auction prices at eBay, for example, and the prices offered on Amazon. With wireless Internet for your laptop or phone, you can look at current prices while browsing piles of 25-cent books at rummage sales, and cherry-pick the easiest profit makers. Some sellers price books at a penny on Amazon, counting on their share (roughly $1.70) of the $3.99 shipping charge to cover postage and a small profit. It's a risky strategy. Stick to popular books that sell for several dollars more than you pay.

Where do you get the books? I just read the story of a man who got his first 8,000 books for $100, buying the leftovers at a "Friends of the Library" sale. He sold $10,000 of them at last count. Check thrift stores, rummage sales, and

117

flea markets too. How much potential is there? Look at some used books on Amazon.com and you'll see sellers with more than 600,000 customer ratings. Those are just the sales where the customer bothered to rate the seller. Of the thousands of used booksellers indexed by Manta.com, about 180 have estimated annual revenues of $1 million or more.

How to Get Started

Sell a book online. This first step provides momentum and experience. Then invest as little as $100 into select books. Unlike with bookstores at a physical location, where customers are enticed by a large inventory, nobody cares how many books you have when you sell online. If you have the title they want, they buy it. You may later find a niche you like and are better at. One bookseller makes $1,000 weekly specializing in rare books he auctions on eBay. He pays up to $20 for books he sells for as much as $100, but even he recommends that beginners pay no more than a dollar for any one book.

Resources

- *The Home-Based Bookstore: Start Your Own Business Selling Used Books on Amazon, eBay or Your Own Web Site* by Steve Weber (Weber Books, 2005).
- www.sellbackyourbook.com: Enter the book's ISBN to see if this company will buy your book or textbook.
- www.sellyourbooksonline.com: Information on how to sell books online.
- www.weberbooks.com/selling: An example of a successful used bookseller.
- http://stores.ebay.com/cookbookstore: An eBay cookbook store.

CHAPTER 49

SELL YOUR DATING, DESIGN, OR DOG EXPERTISE

SPECIALTY CONSULTING

A coworker at a small Native American–owned casino where I worked many years ago quit to become a consultant. He had worked all the table games and had been in various management positions, so he had the knowledge and experience necessary to advise small tribes that wanted to start or expand a casino operation on their reservations. I don't know how he did in his new career, but his story demonstrates how specialized a consulting niche can be. Alan Weiss, the author of *Million Dollar Consulting*, says, "The horrible news about consulting is that there is no barrier to entry. The great news about consulting is that there is no barrier to entry." In other words, competition can be intense in some fields, but anyone can become a consultant in a niche with less competition—and with virtually no legal requirements or investment. You can sell your services to others based on *your* particular expertise, and we're all experts on something.

Examples of niches in which people hire consultants include dating, efficiency, dog breeding, health, social media marketing . . . the list goes on. The point is to provide expertise that the client needs and doesn't have. An art consultant, for example, is paid to help individuals or businesses decide which pieces of art to buy. This could be for the purpose of creating a personal collection, an investment portfolio, or a themed interior design plan for a hotel chain. If you know how to build log cabins, you might sell on-site consultation services, or charge $100 per hour for phone and e-mail consultations.

Money

Fees vary greatly. Top marketing consultants charge thousands of dollars per hour, for example, while a home-decorating consultant might make $40 per hour.

119

I once paid a business consultant just $50 for two hours and learned that you get what you pay for. The hourly or project rate is not the only consideration. Small niches have very little competition, making it easier for a newcomer. Of course, unless you plan to get educated and trained in a high-fee field (not a bad idea), you're limited to niches in which you already have more knowledge than most.

Of the hundreds of thousands of consultants and consulting companies in the United States, most make less than $1 million in annual revenue, but several thousand manage to do more than $20 million per year.

How to Get Started

Choose an area of expertise in which you have knowledge and experience and will enjoy sharing it. If your friends all envy your perfect flower garden, for example, charge $30 per hour to advise clients on flower garden design and care. With local competition, you have a basis for pricing. Otherwise, it's up to you to convince clients what your service is worth. Car-buying consultants can easily justify a $100 to $300 fee for finding a client a car if they save the client more than that. In many niches you'll have to guess and test to determine prices. Think about how a client actually benefits from your expertise, and make that clear in your marketing.

Resources

- *Consulting For Dummies,* Second edition, by Bob Nelson and Peter Economy (Wiley Publishing, 2008): Covers everything from how to start to promoting your business and negotiating contracts.
- *Getting Started in Consulting,* Third edition, by Alan Weiss (John Wiley & Sons, Inc., 2009).
- www.idealist.org/if/as/Consultant: A searchable database of consultants; a good place to be listed.
- www.consultantmoms.com: An example of a consulting company in the home party sales niche.

CHAPTER 50

STAYING HOME
MONDAY MORNING

VIRTUAL ASSISTANT

Make up to $35 per hour staying home? You bet. If you're proficient with basic secretarial and computer-related work, you can work from the spare room in your house as a virtual assistant (VA). You can do it as an employee or start your own business. You'll be helping out busy people who don't have the time for many things they need to do but who also don't want to hire a full-time employee. Depending on experience and knowledge, you can offer a variety of services. You might do customer service work by phone or e-mail, write letters, make appointments, set up interviews, make reminder calls, prepare reports, and much more. A writer may need eight hours of research work done for his book. A web site owner could need link exchanges arranged. A busy executive might want someone to order flowers for his wife and help his kids with their homework by e-mail.

You can do any and all of the things clients want, or you can choose to specialize in certain areas. Some virtual assistants focus on work related to web-based businesses, like putting up pages, preparing e-mail newsletters, and processing customer orders or complaints. It is up to you which way you want to go in this business.

Money

Virtual assistant services in India and the Philippines charge as little as $4 per hour, but fortunately many clients prefer a VA based in the United States or Canada. A few North American virtual assistants charge $10 per hour, but $15 to $35 is the norm, and the higher end is common. What you can charge depends on your skills. Web design skills are in high demand, and familiarity

121

with online marketing can help boost that rate as well. If you want to grow your business to include employees, you have to charge a rate that allows a decent profit after your employee cost.

If you prefer the simplicity of a one-person business, learn the skills necessary to charge $35 per hour. Then get enough clients and you'll have a decent annual income. Having set rates for certain tasks is another option, and that allows you to make $50 per hour or more if you're efficient. What can you make if you hire employees? Although a relatively new field, data on U.S. companies that provide virtual assistants indicates that several of them top $1 million in annual sales.

How to Get Started

If you already have a computer with Internet access and a phone line you can designate for business, you have the basic tools of a virtual assistant. A scanner, fax machine, and software programs can be bought as needed. You'll need a web site, and it should look good, especially if you are offering web design or web marketing services. A free PayPal account is sufficient for processing payments.

More predictable income comes with regular clients, but to start you can go to freelance sites like Elance.com and bid on various jobs to generate some income quickly and possibly get some repeat business. For example, I'll soon be hiring a freelancer to research 100 topics for me, and if he or she does good work, I might use that person as a virtual assistant on a regular basis.

Resources

- *The Virtual Assistant Handbook: Insider Secrets for Starting and Running Your Own Profitable VA Business* by Nadine Hill (Lean Marketing Press, 2009).
- www.virtualassistants.com: Lists virtual assistants and jobs in the field.
- www.txvirtualassistant.com: An example of a virtual assistant in Texas.

PART SEVEN

WORKING WITH PEOPLE

To be honest, I'm not really a people person. I was once employed supervising adults with developmental disabilities, and although I got good reviews from both my employer and my clients, I had to quit after several months—and not just because that was the usual job duration for me. Let's just say I'm very happy there are people who like this and other social work. Being a convention host, collection agent, and sample distributor definitely involved dealing with a lot of people, and these jobs served their purpose for me, too, but I noticed that unlike myself, other employees truly loved the fact that they got to work with people so much.

If you're like them, this section has some interesting selections for you. Did you know that you can travel the world teaching people English, or make a business of helping senior citizens move into new homes? You can also be a bartender on a cruise ship or help people organize their garages and closets. Some of these jobs and businesses have real income potential as well.

MIKE KOPCZYNSKI, BARTENDER

Mike Kopczynski is a bartender currently working in Cañon City, Colorado. Over the years he has tended bar in everything from a strip club to an Irish pub. I asked him a few questions about how he started and what he likes about the job. Wait until you read how he got his first job bartending. Sometimes it pays to be bold.

What was the first bartending job that you had, and how did you get hired?

Well, I had just moved back to Myrtle Beach, South Carolina. I was looking for work doing just about anything when a friend of mine suggested going into the Crazy Horse. It was an upscale adult strip club. Thinking I had nothing to lose and in the mood for a little joke, I walked in and said,

"My name is Mike, and I am supposed to start work today. I am your new bar-back." The manager looked confused and went to the office to look for my paperwork. After a few minutes, he came back with an application and tax forms. He informed me that he couldn't find any of my information and instructed me to fill out another application and see the bar manager for my uniform. After bar-backing for just over three months, I became a full-time bartender. I worked there for over two years.

How many bartending jobs have you had over the years, and in how many different cities?

I have always been a traveler at heart, so I have had quite a few jobs in many cities—Myrtle Beach, South Carolina; Nashville, Tennessee; Huntsville, Alabama; Vail, Colorado; Glendale, Arizona; Bethlehem, Pennsylvania; and Cañon City, Colorado. I would say close to 10 jobs in all.

You've worked for two of Jimmy Buffett's Margaritaville restaurants. Was that a fun environment to work in?

It was an absolute blast. It hardly ever felt like I was working. I was simply showing up to have fun every day.

As a bartender, do you ever get benefits like health insurance or paid vacation time?

I have had insurance with a few jobs. Corporate restaurants are where to apply if you are looking for insurance and vacation time. While at Margaritaville, I received Blue Cross Blue Shield health, dental, and vision insurance, as well as paid vacation. Bartending jobs at Outback Steakhouse, Applebee's, and places like that also have these benefits.

I assume that a bartender makes most of his money from customer tips. What is the most you have made in a night between wages and tips?

There was one day I will always remember. I was scheduled to open Margaritaville in Glendale, Arizona, and ended up working a double shift as a bartender had called out sick. I bartended from 11 AM till 2 AM. That day I brought home over $700 in tips and also collected 15 hours of pay at $4.25 an hour.

From your experience, how much would you say a bartender can make weekly at a busy or upscale bar or club?

I would say at an upscale bar or restaurant a bartender should easily make over $1,000 a week, although some places do shift in and out of busy seasons.

I understand that you are learning how to brew beer at the pub you currently work in. That could lead to a whole new career. In your experience, is it generally possible for a bartender to move into other positions within a company—perhaps including management or marketing—if he or she is motivated and wants that?

Yes, of course. A friend of mine who I bartended with in Myrtle Beach has just recently been transferred to another city and has been promoted to bar manager. There is always room for a bartender to get promoted to management positions.

What do you like about the job and what advice can you offer to potential bartenders?

Never think you can't do it or that you don't have the personality. Never get intimidated that you don't know the drinks. I have never met a bartender who knows how to make everything. When I first started out at my very first bar, I faked everything and was constantly learning.

The best thing about being a bartender is the people you meet while doing your job. You never know who is going to sit in front of you.

CHAPTER 51

HANDICAPPED KIDS AND OTHER DAY-CARE NICHES

SPECIALTY DAY CARE

Despite the many thousands of day-care businesses out there, people sometimes still can't find one that works for them. Why? Because they have special needs. I knew a woman who worked a late shift, for example, and didn't finish until 3:00 AM. None of the area day-care services kept those hours, so she paid a friend to keep her son overnight. In some towns parents of children with disabilities can't find appropriate care. Those are two examples of niches you can serve if you want to start a day-care business.

Other possibilities include taking in only infants or only older children. There are day-care centers just for elderly folks as well. Some people keep their aging parents living with them but can't be home to care for them on workdays. In some cities, enough demand might exist for day care for adults with developmental disabilities. What's the biggest advantage of serving these niche markets? With less competition, you can get clients more easily and/or charge higher fees.

Money

Child-care workers average only $20,940 annually, and although that average is more than $24,000 in California, Massachusetts, New York, and the District of Columbia, this is obviously not great employment from an income perspective. A job, of course, is business training if you treat it as such.

The rates you can charge in your own business depend on where you are and what you offer. In Washington, D.C., for example, parents pay up to $200 weekly per child, while in other parts of the country rates start as low as $75 per week. Targeting a special niche lets you charge higher rates because there is less competition. It also lowers the risk starting out. You're more likely to get customers right away if you're the only nighttime provider in the area, for example. What's the profit potential with your own business? Recent statistics show at least 200 day-care providers that do $1 million or more in annual revenue. That level of success requires more than one location, but you, too, can eventually expand to new locations or franchise your winning business formula.

How to Get Started

Unless you've already worked in day care or have had a house full of kids for years, it's best to work as an employee for a while, or volunteer at a day-care center run by a church or nonprofit organization. The experience will let you know if you really like this type of work. It is also a way to determine which niche you might want to target when you start your business.

You need an appropriate location for a day-care center. If local zoning and regulations allow it, you can start with your home to lower your investment risk. Check for any other local rules regarding day-care or child-care services, like mandated staff-to-child ratios. Every state regulates child care now as well, so you'll have to check on the licensing requirements and rules for your state.

Resources

- *How to Start a Home Based Daycare* by Shari Steelsmith (Globe Pequot, 2003): Advice from someone in the business, and forms you can use.
- www.naccrra.org: A trade association for child-care businesses and workers; provides online training and credentials.
- www.childcare.net: Information on how to start a day-care business.
- www.childcare24hours.com: Example of a service that provides nighttime child care.
- http://nccic.acf.hhs.gov: Many resources, including links to licensing information for all states.

CHAPTER 52

THE LIFE OF A TRAVELING BARTENDER

DRINK SERVER

Bartending is not an unusual way to make money, but it offers some benefits you don't find in most jobs. First, it is a great survival job. Once you have experience you can almost always find a position quickly. More than 400,000 bartending jobs exist in the United States at the moment, and turnover is high. Even small towns have openings almost weekly. The second benefit comes from the first: You can travel or live where you want and quickly find work. You can even move to an exotic locale overseas, or work on a cruise ship or at a luxury resort.

As I write this, Jimmy Buffett's Margaritaville.com has job openings listed for its restaurants in Panama City, Florida; Glendale, Arizona; Myrtle Beach, South Carolina; Las Vegas; and more. The web site CruiseShipJob.com has several listings for bartending positions on cruise ships. Travel destinations that attract a lot of Americans are another good place to look for bartending jobs.

Money

The Bureau of Labor Statistics shows just $20,300 as the average wage of bartending positions—a bit more than dishwashing. That's nonsense, and the reason is clear: Bartenders don't report all of their tips. At the moment, the minimum wage for tipped employees is $2.13 an hour, and although many employers pay more, it is typical for bartenders to report only enough of their tips to show $9 or $10 per hour when added to their base rate.

Income varies widely according to where you work and the shifts you get. To make more money, look for jobs in busy, expensive bars, clubs, and restaurants, and try to get night and weekend shifts. Someday starting your own bar is the way to really cash in, of course. If you own a bar or club, the sky is the limit. Even a small bar can net $100,000 annually, and almost 200 nightclubs in the United States do $5 million or more in annual revenue. For an idea of what's possible as an employee, see the interview with Mike Kopczynski.

How to Get Started

Bartending schools and online courses that provide certification (an inexpensive one is listed in the resources section) can help, but the best qualification is experience. You can get that at smaller bars, restaurants, and clubs. You can also start as a bar-back, an assistant bartender who stocks things, runs for supplies, and helps in any way necessary. A bar-back is typically paid a base rate and a share of the bartender's tips.

Of course, it helps to know a few drinks before applying, so buy a good drink guide. But don't think you're going to memorize the thousand drink recipes in it. Bring the book to a bartender friend (make one if necessary) and have him or her mark the 30 most commonly ordered drinks. Memorize those. To get a feel for the kind of establishment you want to work in, and where the tips are better, visit several different types of bars, talking to the bartenders and taking notes. This is job preparation you can enjoy.

Resources

- *Bartending For Dummies,* Fourth edition, by Ray Foley (Wiley Publishing, 2010).
- www.makemoneybartending.com: Check out the articles here on how to increase tips—something not covered in most "how to bartend" books.
- http://bartending.com: Resources for bartenders. Also has an inexpensive online bartending course that comes with certification.
- www.cruiseshipjob.com: Listings of jobs on cruise ships, including bartending positions.
- http://forum.drinksmixer.com: A discussion forum where bartenders exchange tips, news, and ideas.

CHAPTER 53

PROFESSOR WITHOUT A DEGREE

NONCREDIT COLLEGE TEACHER

The owner of a spiritual bookstore where we used to live had a class at the local community college on "past life regression." She probably saw a decent increase in sales at her store thanks to this course, since she continued it for years. My father, an attorney, taught a course on workers' compensation law at a college years ago. He collected a portion of the course fee from the dozen attendees (mostly insurance agents), and he recalls getting at least one case as a result of the class. These noncredit or *continuing education* classes are offered at many community colleges. Students are there for the knowledge, not for credit toward a degree, so the teachers do not necessarily need to meet any legal or certification requirements. As I write this, my accountant is offering a course at the local college on using Quick-Books, the software accounting program.

Other noncredit classes I've seen advertised include flower arranging, cave exploration, real estate investing, entrepreneurship, basket weaving, and many more. Sometimes these are one-night classes, and others take place several times weekly for two weeks or more. Each college has its own fee-sharing plan, but most who teach these courses do so for their passion and to promote their businesses. If you lost 100 pounds, for example, and now own a gym, you could teach a course on weight control through physical conditioning, and you might get some new customers for your business.

Money

Some colleges will give you half of the course fee. Others keep a minimum amount to cover the use of the room and then split revenues beyond that. Keep half of the fees from your one-night $50 course on writing résumés with 14 students, and you would make $350. Nice pay for a few hours work but not much if you do this only once per semester. Here are some examples of recent classes and prices for a community college in Arizona: Franchising, one two-hour class for $45; Introduction to the Internet, two two-hour classes for $99; Marketing: From Product to Profit, one two-hour class for $10; Spa Etiquette Training Program (for spa/beauty industry professionals), four two-hour classes for $500. Classes like that last one show the potential in obscure niches.

Some teachers boost revenues by requiring the purchase of study materials they produce—or at least offering them for sale. But again, most classes are part of a larger marketing plan for a business the teacher already has.

How to Get Started

If you just want to share your knowledge and make some extra cash, teach a subject you're passionate about. To make more money, create a class that will help promote your book or business. Some colleges have forms you can download online to make a proposal. With others you can send a letter explaining the course curriculum, why you are the right person to teach it, and how many students you anticipate. Your class will be listed in those offered by the college, but you might supplement that with classified advertising or fliers posted in appropriate places.

Resources

- *Make Money Teaching Online: How to Land Your First Academic Job, Build Credibility, and Earn a Six-Figure Salary* by Danielle Babb and Jim Mirabella (John Wiley & Sons, Inc., 2007): Aimed at those with experience and/or teaching certifications but provides many new ways to make teaching pay.
- http://makemoneyteaching.com: Covers several ways to make money teaching without a degree.
- http://prairiestate.edu/ced/descriptions.html: An example of noncredit classes available from a state college.

CHAPTER 54

COMING INTO THE CLOSET

HOME-ORGANIZING CONSULTANT

If your home is a disaster, just skip to the next chapter. A home-organizing consultant has to be neat and, well . . . organized. No surprise there. Now if your friends make fun of or compliment you on how everything is in its place in your home, and you like the idea of helping other people overcome the clutter in their garages, bedrooms, kitchens, and closets, this might be an ideal business for you. You can run it from home, meaning low overhead, and you can start with $2,000 or less in supplies and marketing.

The niches are perhaps more interesting, and have less competition. You might specialize in organizing home offices, for example. Or you might do just garages and sheds. Some people might even need help with their cars. Kitchens are a big problem for many, so you might have a Just Kitchens organizing company.

Money

Quite a few home-organizing companies are large enough to have employees now, but the pay is about what you would expect. The bigger potential is always in starting your own business. Many home-organizing consultants offer a free quote and charge by the job. They look at the home and talk to the owner, and then specify in writing the price and what is included. The goal should be to make $25 to $35 per hour. Simply charging these hourly rates is one way to price your service, but the advantages of a quoted per-job price are the customer's comfort of knowing exactly what the price will be and your ability to boost your hourly profit with efficient work. Additional profits come from selling shelves, storage containers, and other products that help the client stay organized. Having these in stock can add to inventory costs, but they sell themselves if you have them on hand during the cleanup.

Entrepreneur magazine says of this business, "an income of $40,000 per year is easily attainable." Whether easily or not, many companies in the home-organizing market have done far better than that. Recent statistics show more than a hundred that gross over $1 million annually.

How to Get Started

If you intend to charge by the job, practice doing estimates for a few friends and then actually do the jobs for them (perhaps at a discount) to see if you hit your hourly pay goal. You don't want to discover on a large job that you're making only minimum wage. Learning to estimate is important because even if you charge by the hour customers still want some idea of how much they will have to pay in total. Prepare a portfolio to show them, with before and after photos of previous jobs, along with a description of the work done and the final charge.

If you are uncertain about starting a business like this on your own, some franchise opportunities are available (see the resources section), even in the more specialized niches. The advantages to paying for a franchise are having a system that has proved successful and getting support from people in the business.

Resources

- *Smart Closet Makeovers* by the editors of Sunset Books (Oxmoor House, 2006): Meant for do-it-yourselfers but full of ideas you can use.
- www.garageenvy.com: A garage organization consulting and sales company.
- www.clutterfreeservices.com: A general home-organizing company in the San Francisco area.
- www.closetandstorageconcepts.com: A closet-organizing company since 1987; it offers franchises.

CHAPTER 55

STUDENTS PAY YOU
$50 PER HOUR

SPECIALIZED TUTOR

If you've worked in schools previously, the idea of being a tutor has probably occurred to you. But those of you without a teaching certificate or degree can do this as well. The job carries no legal requirements, and the bottom line is that customer satisfaction is your qualification. Your students either benefit or they stop using your service. If you know any subject well, you can find clients. If you know several subjects well enough, you can choose your niche. You can tutor English, math, art, languages, business, music, computer skills, writing, science, sports, and history. Other possibilities include special needs tutoring jobs, college preparation tutoring positions, and even overseas jobs tutoring the children of American businessmen and diplomats.

In some circumstances, such as tutoring children of embassy employees, you might work in a room that's provided for you. Most of the time you will work in the home of the client. You can also set aside space in your own home to tutor students. If you are flexible and work well with people, you can make a decent income as a tutor and make really good money if you someday expand into a business with other employees.

Money

Rates vary both by locale and subject matter. On one web site that represents more than 27,000 tutors, the lowest rate I found was $20 per hour for Spanish language tutoring in Pueblo, Colorado. With a population that is 39 percent Hispanic, there are probably a lot of qualified tutors to compete against. On the other hand, math tutors in Pueblo are all asking $40 per hour. In New York City the hourly rate for math tutoring ranges from $50 to $85.

For test-preparation tutoring, the rate can be as high as $100 per hour if you have a good reputation.

If you use a web site that helps you find business (see the resources section), it will typically advertise to bring in potential clients, direct those in your locale to you, and collect payment for you. For this, it will keep 20 to 40 percent of the hourly rate charged. If you're concerned about its share cutting into your pay, just set the rate high enough to get what you want after paying the percentage. You can make decent money doing this yourself, but if you really want the big money, start hiring others to tutor. How much could you make? Educate Inc., parent company of Sylvan Learning Centers, makes more than $100 million annually.

How to Get Started

Although there are not legal requirements, clients often prefer that you have some qualifications, certifications, or experience. One of the advantages of working through an online facilitator is that it can certify you. On wyzant .com, for example, many tutors are certified in 10 or more subjects. You get these certifications either by passing online tests that the facilitator provides (one chance only) or by providing evidence of previous experience and qualifications. Even if you don't get much business through a service like this, by using its system you can honestly say in your own marketing materials that you are certified in certain subjects by that organization.

Resources

- *How to Start a Home-Based Tutoring Business* by Beth Lewis (Globe Pequot, 2010): Advice, checklists, invoices, and more.
- www.pnwlocalnews.com/south_king/aub/news/38628819.html: A story about a woman who made up to $100 per hour tutoring.
- www.tutoringservices.com: A free meeting place for tutors and clients.
- www.wyzant.com: Offers free registration for tutors; it then takes a percentage for arranging jobs and processing payments.

CHAPTER 56

PREPPING GRANDPA'S CONDO

SENIOR SERVICES PROVIDER

The senior population in America is expected to double by 2030, and many of our older citizens need help. Some will have to downsize to a condo or smaller house, and family members can be too busy to help or too overwhelmed with the process. A senior move specialist can arrange the move, sell household items, prepare the new home for special needs, and provide related services. That's one example of many services you can offer if you have the desire and compassion needed to get into this industry.

Seniors need rides to the store if they no longer drive. They need pets taken to the vet. They need help arranging homes for easy wheelchair and scooter access. You can offer bathing, grooming, dressing, medical reminders, housekeeping, errands, meal preparation, general supervision, bill paying, laundry, pet care, and much more. Services like these can make it possible for the elderly to stay in their own or family homes, saving them (or their family) from the much more expensive option of nursing home care. As an owner of a senior services business, you can offer all these services or specialize in one of the many niches.

Money

Prices vary according to the locale and the level of service. With health care certifications (CNA—certified nursing assistant, for example) you can charge more for those who need more care. The elderly look at not only at the value of retaining more independence but also the relative cost advantages of in-home care versus a nursing home. The average annual cost of the latter is more than $70,000, or $1,350 per week. If a senior services company can provide the necessary help that allows an elderly person to stay home for $300 or $600 weekly, that represents a huge savings.

The going rate in most areas of the country is $20 to $30 hourly for many senior services, including cleaning, running errands (mileage charges are extra), or just checking up on a client. Since many seniors need only a couple of hours of help daily, a charge of $25 per hour might total less than $400 weekly—much cheaper than a nursing home. Fill your schedule and you can make $50,000 annually. Grow your company to include employees, and you can someday have one of the many senior services that make more than $1 million in annual revenue.

How to Get Started

Working in the field is a good way to start. Nursing assistants average about $12 per hour. As an employee of a company providing in-home care, you might make less than that, but the training and experience can help you prepare to start your own business. Getting certified as a CNA if you plan to do a lot of the work yourself will allow you to charge more.

Do some market research to see what services are most in demand in your area and which have the least competition. Then you can decide whether to offer anything and everything or to specialize in a particular niche.

Resources

- *Start Your Own Senior Services Business: Adult Day Care, Relocation Services, Homecare, Transportation Service, Concierge, Travel Service and More,* Second edition, by Charlene Davis (Entrepreneur Press, 2010): A guide to choosing your niche and starting your business in the senior services industry.
- http://savvyseniorbillpay.com: An example of a senior services business that focuses on bill paying and other financial tasks.
- www.comforcare.com: A successful provider of senior home care that now offers franchises.
- www.yourcnatrainingguide.com: Information on getting certified as a CNA.

CHAPTER 57

PAID TO TRAVEL THE WORLD

ENGLISH TEACHER OVERSEAS

Take any bachelor's degree, add a simple certification, and you can see the world while teaching English. But first, let's get a bunch of acronyms out of the way. As you check out the opportunities, you'll see the following mentioned: ESL (English as a Second Language), EFL (English as a Foreign Language), TESL (Teaching English as a Second Language), TESOL (Teaching English to Students of Other Languages), and TEFL (Teaching English as a Foreign Language). TESL, TESOL, and TEFL are used somewhat interchangeably.

Many employers prefer you to have some experience teaching ESL. The job can involve anything from tutoring young children to working with business professionals who need to learn English before (or after) coming to the United States. A wide variety of organizations hire for these positions. Some employers will pay for your plane ticket if you sign a contract for a year. However, they generally won't pay for the return ticket, so consider your destination carefully.

Money

Pay is best where demand is high, competition is low, and wages in general are healthy. At the moment, this means Japan. Check around, though, as the rates of pay change according to an evolving market, political developments, and currency exchange rates. In any case, there might be places you will want to live for a while regardless of pay. A recent check of listings for ESL jobs showed a range from $3.60 per hour in Peru to $2,900 per month teaching English in Japan.

If it is more money you're looking for, starting your own English-teaching school is another way to go. Or you can train others for these

English-teaching positions. TEFL International, an Oregon company, does that, and Manta.com estimates its annual revenue at more than $1 million.

How to Get Started

Some employers do not require a college degree as long as you are a native English speaker, have some experience, and have a TESL certificate. But many do require a bachelor's degree. It does not have to be in education, as long as it is supplemented with a TESL, TEFL, or other relevant certification. You can get certified in a number of ways. Online courses cost as little as $149 and can take just two or three weeks to complete. You can find an example in the resources section, but many good companies and schools offer certification courses. Certification gained through more intensive courses or those that are obtained overseas may be valued more highly by employers. Training overseas where you hope to work is not a bad idea in any case.

Employers will usually choose applicants with experience, so why not get some? That's not as difficult as it may sound. Churches, nonprofit organizations, and even government employment agencies are often looking for volunteers to teach English to immigrants. Offer to work for them for a few hours once a week, and in two seasons you can honestly say that you have six months of experience.

Resources

- *Teaching English Overseas: A Job Guide for Americans and Canadians,* Third edition, by Jeff Mohamed (English International, 2003): Not too recent, but most other TESL books target British readers.
- www.linguaedge.com: Offers several teaching certificate courses (TESOL, TESL, TEFL).
- www.needateacher.com: Easy-to-navigate job listings from around the world.
- http://coinmill.com: A currency converter to show what you're really getting paid.
- www.tefllife.com: TEFL courses in Nepal, Egypt, Vietnam, and 16 other countries, and job placement services.

PART EIGHT

WORKING WITH ANIMALS

My wife, Ana, and I love our two cats. We had the whole backyard cat-proofed so they can enjoy outdoor time without danger from local coyotes, mountain lions, and foxes. We buy them the best food. They're the photogenic stars of a Spanish-language web site Ana created. They make our life richer. So as much as I wouldn't want the responsibility of dozens of animals, I can understand the desire many people have to work with them. And yes, in my distant past I have even made money babysitting or walking or washing a dog or two.

This section is for animal lovers. The jobs and businesses here are not all that unusual any longer, but there are still some interesting niches that you won't find in the local employment listings. You may not have thought of becoming a Komodo dragon trainer for Disney, for example, or of building enclosures for cats that allow them to be outdoors safely. And you might make some real money running a specialized boarding house for any and all animals, or a pet taxi service.

LISA KELLY, KITTY CAT CONDOS

Lisa Kelly liked to travel but did not like the idea of her cat being stuck in a small metal cage at a veterinarian or a dog kennel. That dissatisfaction with the cat boarding options available motivated her to start Kitty Cat Condos in Portland, Oregon, more than 15 years ago. Her facility is a cat-only operation that specializes in more luxurious accommodations than are available at most boarding facilities.

How long were you in business before you were able to make a decent living at it?

Four to five years, but I started when cat boarding was not common. Most people left some food out or had a neighbor come by and check on [their pets].

Many cats in our area were outdoor/farm cats, and there's not much demand for boarding outdoor cats. Or the indoor cats that did get boarded usually boarded at their local vet's office, since no cat kennels were available at the time.

How do you get most of your business?

Word of mouth from owners telling or bragging to friends; we used to send home photos of the cats if we caught them in cute poses in the rooms and stamp our name on the photo. That way when they share with friends at the office, etc. . . . and they do . . . they see our name and the conversation usually comes up. . . . The other biggest is vet offices, but that did not come easy. Most vets considered me competition in the beginning. Until they started to send me their problem cats—ones that are mean or extremely stressed when boarding. Then, once many of them saw the cats did way better in our environment, they were amazed and many decided to stop the cat boarding business and just send them to us since they realized how well the horrible boarders did in a roomlike structure. Many of these cats would not eat or use the box while being boarded in a vet cage, especially with all the stress and dogs barking and horrible sounds of sick recovering animals, many become sick in this type of situation. So with all the issues plus the cost of a staff to care for the cats on the weekends, many vets in our area decided it just was not worth the $10 a day.

Are there many licensing or other legal requirements to start a kennel, and do these impose much cost or trouble?

We were grandfathered in 14 to 15 years ago because cats did not need land use permits—only dogs did. But now with the economy, I believe the city officials are allowing more since there tends to be a doggie day care on every corner; so my guess is it is easier than ever to get a kennel approval but not sure as I came in under old rules.

Assuming that a person could start this business in her own home, would you say it is possible to start with $1,000?

Not sure. . . . Would really depend on how many individual spaces you would have or start with and what type of furnishings etc. in the rooms.

Do you offer other products and services besides taking care of cats for their owners?

Yes. We are offering all the products for pets traveling, especially by airline. This part of our company has doubled each year. More and more people bring pets along instead of boarding, now that all the pet-friendly hotels are available.

CHAPTER 58

HOOKING UP LADY AND THE TRAMP

DOG BREEDER

When people see puppies going for the cost of vaccinations at animal shelters, and then hear about ones that sell for $500, they think big money is to be had in dog breeding. But when you go online to discussion forums where dog breeders meet, it seems that few do it for the money, or even make money when they try. It can cost $2,000 to rear a litter of four or five Shetland sheepdog pups properly, and at a sale price of $400 to $500 each, that means roughly breaking even. Granted, some breeds sell for much more. English bulldog puppies are selling for $800 to $2,250 in most parts of the United States, for example. But the big profits in general breeding are made at what are called *puppy mills*, and this money comes at the expense of poor treatment of the animals.

What can you do, then, if you like the idea of making some money breeding dogs and doing so humanely? Stick to niches where you can combine breeding with training of dogs that are truly needed by people. Certain breeds work best as guide dogs for the blind, for example, but they need intensive training. Other breeds are used for herding sheep or cattle, or for sniffing out drugs. The addition of training allows you to make money while properly caring for your dogs so you can avoid the cruelty that's often a part of "efficient breeding."

Money

Prices vary widely according to the dog breed as well as the type and level of training needed. For example, herding-dog puppies like Australian shepherds are sold for around $600 without training but much more when trained. One breeder and trainer who prepares border collies for goose control work sells the dogs for $3,000 to $6,500 each. German shepherds, Labrador retrievers, and golden retrievers are used as seeing-eye dogs for the blind, and their purchase is usually subsidized. In this field you can also make money working for or running one of the nonprofit organizations that supplies the dogs. German shepherds, Labrador retrievers, and Belgian shepherds are the most common police dogs, used for jobs like drug or explosives detection. Fully trained, they sell for $5,000 to $8,000 each.

How to Get Started

Working for an organization that trains guide dogs for the deaf and blind is a way to get into the field as an employee. Jobs with farms and companies that train dogs for other purposes can provide the necessary experience to someday start your own business. Avoid puppy mills that provide minimal care to maximize profits on animals. Even if you have no moral qualms about making money in that way, such outfits are not stable businesses because they often get fined or shut down for cruelty to animals.

Although you will rarely find formal requirements for employment with dog breeders, it helps to have some experience handling animals. A way to easily get that experience is to locate one of the many animal shelters that need volunteers to walk their dogs. This can also help you decide if you like working with animals enough to make it a career or business.

Resources

- *The Complete Book of Dog Breeding,* Second edition, by Dan Rice (Barron's Educational Series, 2008).
- www.highlandcanine.com: A seller and trainer of dogs for herding, protection, search and rescue, explosives detection, and more.
- www.dogbreedinfo.com: Hundreds of pages of information about dogs and breeding.
- www.seeingeye.org: An organization that breeds and trains seeing-eye dogs.

CHAPTER 59

MAKING PETS BEAUTIFUL

MOBILE PET GROOMER

Dog-grooming businesses have been around since at least the 1800s, and other animal grooming services for almost as long. Up until recently, though, people generally had to bring their pets to a groomer's place of business, which can be inconvenient for the customer and also means a long ride to a strange place for the animal. For these reasons, many pet owners are willing to pay a little extra to have the groomer come to them. If you love working with animals, you can be the one making those house calls.

Dogs and cats are the primary pets you'll be grooming. Some services advertise horse grooming, too, and there is no reason you can't wash and comb the hair of people's bunnies and other animals. You can start with relatively simple tools, and do this work in the homes of clients. Later you can get a fully equipped pet-grooming trailer and bring everything you need right to their driveway. Your services can include nail cutting, washing, haircuts, accessorizing, and more.

Money

Demand for pet grooming is growing, and there is only one groomer for every 4,000 dogs and cats. Many towns have no mobile pet-grooming services, so this can be a lucrative niche with little competition. Grooming and a haircut for a dog can run from $30 to $100. That can include bathing, nail trimming, ear and eye cleaning, brushing hair, brushing teeth, anal gland expressing, and blow-drying of hair after washing, or these things can be charged for separately as needed. You can offer other services, such as de-matting of fur ($7 to $9), application of flea-killing shampoo or powder ($3 to $10), and pet massage ($10 to $30). Some companies charge extra for clients who are more than

10 miles away. Grooming prices for other animals vary even more, with bigger charges for horses than for pet pigs, for example.

If you love the work, you might choose to keep it simple and just make a living as an owner-operator. If, however, you want to grow your business you can buy more grooming trailers and hire employees at some point. A handful of pet-grooming businesses make more than $1 million in annual revenue.

How to Get Started

You can choose from a couple of basic ways to start and run your business. You can first work as an employee. The places most likely to be hiring are the large pet product chain stores that offer grooming services. If they require some experience, you can volunteer to bathe and groom animals for a while at a local animal shelter. Once you're ready to start your business, you can buy basic tools and do the jobs in clients' homes. Have business cards made to distribute to area veterinarians and to post on appropriate bulletin boards.

For a faster start and potentially faster growth of your business, you can invest in a pet-grooming trailer. Some of the companies that sell them also offer training in pet grooming and in the use of their particular equipment. These start at about $20,000, and you'll need a trailer hitch on your car, but your business will look more professional.

Resources

- *The Business Guide to Pet Grooming* by Sam Kohl (Aaronco Publishing, 2005).
- *Dog Grooming For Dummies* by Margaret H. Bonham (Wiley Publishing, 2006).
- www.pet-business-opportunity.com: Pet business information including a pet grooming business plan.
- www.ambersmobilepetsalons.com: Dog-grooming trailers and training.
- www.ocmobilepetsalon.com: Example of a mobile pet-grooming business.

CHAPTER 60

PAID TO VISIT ANIMALS

PET SITTER

My wife and I refuse to leave our cats alone overnight when we travel, and we don't want to bring them to an animal boarding facility. A lot of us treat our pets as children. We're lucky enough to have found a friend who will spend the night with Jack and Opie for $20, all the food he can eat, and a few cans of beer I try to leave for him. Other pet owners we know pay $50 for overnight pet sitting, and we live in a small town.

Staying at clients' houses with their pets is one service you can offer. You can also just check in on the animals once or twice daily to give them food and water. You can watch them in your own home. Fish, birds, rabbits, guinea pigs, and other pets need care as well. Some people want their animals visited each day while they're at work, but the primary reason you'll be hired is that the owners plan to be out of town. Because of that, many pet sitters include related services, like watering plants, opening and closing blinds, and bringing in newspapers and mail.

Money

Overnight sitting is typically priced at $60 or more. Your actual work might involve less than an hour or two of feeding and playing with the pets, so this is a great business if you like to read or have other business work you can do while at the client's house (you could run a web-based business from your laptop, for example). Visits of less than a half hour are normally $15 to $20 each. Once or twice daily you check on the pets, fill food dishes, and—with dogs— let them outside for a few minutes. Holidays typically mean extra charges, whether you're visiting or staying with the pets.

Some sitters take animals into their homes, limiting this to pets from only two or three clients at a time for both safety and to avoid being regulated as a boarding facility. The charges for this are typically $25 to $40 daily, reflecting the lower business cost and other advantages of staying home. At least one company has sitters lined up for this service, taking a cut from each placement. While researching this chapter, I found only nine pet-sitting companies with annual revenues over $500,000, but yours could be the 10th.

How to Get Started

This business is very easy to get into (just ask our friend), but to do it right and charge top dollar you will eventually want to join an organization that offers some credentials as well as access to liability insurance. Initially you can offer your services to friends and family, even before you get business cards printed, which is a good way to determine if you like the work. Have a basic form for customers to fill out, with spaces for any special instructions and the name and phone numbers of family members and the pet's veterinarian.

Resources

- *How to Open and Operate a Financially Successful Pet Sitting Business* by Angela W. Duea (Atlantic Publishing Company, 2008): An Amazon Kindle e-book; you can download a free Kindle reader for your computer at Amazon.com.
- www.petsit.com: Pet Sitters International offers an accreditation program, access to bonding and insurance, and a lot of great information.
- www.cagelessboarding.com: A company that provides pet sitters who watch pets in their homes.
- www.furryfriendpetsitting.com: An example of a pet-sitting service in Massachusetts.

CHAPTER 61

IT'S A WALK IN THE PARK

DOG-WALKER

If you love dogs and want to stay in shape, this business is for you. Dog walkers can start with an investment of a dollar if necessary—the price of some plastic baggies for cleaning up after the animals. People almost always have their own leashes, and word of mouth can be enough to get you your first few jobs. Walks are typically between 20 and 45 minutes, and if you schedule properly and have good dog-handling skills, you can even walk several dogs at once.

To charge higher rates and present yourself as a professional, join one of the dog-walking or pet-sitting organizations that certify you and/or provide cheap liability insurance. Although this business works best in larger cities, it can even provide a part-time income in a smaller town. In general, it is probably more lucrative than it appears, especially if you combine it with other pet-based services.

Money

Typical rates range from $15 to $17 for short walks (15 to 20 minutes) to $18 to $30 for longer walks (30 to 60 minutes). Some dog walkers promise playtime or run time as part of the walk, while many do not specify anything beyond the walk. For second dogs from the same client, it is common to charge just half the rate for the first. Catering to multidog customers is a good profit strategy, since that $20 charge becomes $40 for the same walk if you have three dogs. Discounts for regular service are common, too. If you charge $20 for a 25-minute walk, for example, you might charge $75 for five 15-minute walks weekly. Extra fees are often charged for guaranteed private walks (no other dogs) and for nighttime and very early walks, as well as holiday jobs.

With tight scheduling and walking dogs for multiple clients at once (let them know this is your policy), you can make $40,000 or more annually working five days per week. To make much more you have to expand to include employees, and/or provide related services, like pet sitting and grooming.

How to Get Started

Walk dogs for friends and neighbors, even if you have to do it for free at first to get the experience. Tell them you are going into the business and could use their help referring potential customers to you. Many animal shelters need volunteer dog walkers, which is a good way to get to know many different breeds. Read up on dog handling so you know how to deal with stubborn animals and prevent violent encounters with other dogs. Choose a few good places to walk the dogs, checking them out beforehand.

Let clients know where you walk the dogs and whether you play with them or run with them (ask them if they want this as part of the service). Have business cards made and distribute them to animal groomers, veterinarians, and others who can refer clients to you.

Resources

- *The Dog Walker's Startup Guide: Create Your Own Lucrative Dog Walking Business in 12 Easy Steps* by J.D. Antell (Novus Markets Publishing, 2009): An Amazon Kindle e-book; you can download a free Kindle reader at Amazon.com.
- *How to Run a Dog Business: Putting Your Career Where Your Heart Is* by Veronica Boutelle (Direct Book Service, 2007).
- www.dogwalker.com: Information and a place to advertise your dog-walking service.
- www.chicago-dogwalkers.com: An example of a dog-walking company.
- www.petsitllc.com: An association that provides liability insurance as part of your annual dues.

CHAPTER 62

MANAGING NOAH'S ARK

ANIMAL-BOARDER

There are kennels for dogs, catteries for cats, and friends who take care of your birds or iguanas when you go on vacation. Specialization can work well with pet-based businesses, but another approach is to offer a full-service animal-boarding facility. In other words, why not plan for and take in everything people bring you? Okay, perhaps the violent chimpanzees and venomous snakes are out, but pet hamsters usually come with their own cages and are easy to care for.

This is a great business if you love to be surrounded by animals and interact with them all day and night. You might even be able to do it at home, if you live in an area where the zoning allows it and you have a property that can be properly set up. A big backyard for running dogs helps, and a large pole barn garage can be converted into living spaces for all the various animals you board. If you have a farm property, you might even have room to take care of horses.

Money

At the low end, dogs are boarded for $12 daily, but $18 to $23 is typical; the exact rate is based on the size of the dog and the size of the cage. Some boarding services offer "luxury suites" for as much as $52 daily. Cat boarding starts at around $10 daily, with discounts for additional same-client cats if the cage is shared. Luxury cat boarding runs as high as $22 daily. Animals of similar size can be charged like cats, and small animals that owners bring in their own cages should fall under a minimum charge of $5 to $8 daily. You can charge extra for pet pickup, special treatment, playtime, and walking of pets. Some services also offer cage-free boarding in their homes, although this option is likely to work only if you do it with one or two compatible animals at a time.

At an average of $15 daily, and assuming your kennel has a dozen animals at any one time, your gross revenue would top $5,000 monthly. At least 100 animal boarding companies in the United States make $1 million or more in annual revenue.

How to Get Started

Take in the pets of friends who are traveling to see if you're ready to care for animals day and night. If you feel this business might be right for you, call or visit a few kennels in your area to see how they operate and how much they charge. In particular, see if any of them are full at times, which indicates enough demand for another service.

Although you might start out by pet sitting in your home, to make more income you'll need to invest money for construction of proper facilities and/ or to lease a building if you can't operate from home. Animal-boarding businesses are licensed in most areas now, so check with your local government to see what the requirements are.

Resources

- *Running Your Own Boarding Kennels: The Complete Guide to Kennel and Cattery Management* by David Cavill (Kogan Page, 2008): Focuses on dogs and cats, but the same principles apply to other animal boarding.
- www.kittycondos.com: A cat-boarding kennel in Oregon; a good example of how to run the business and the web site to go with it.
- www.rabbitrescue.com/boarding.html: A bunny-boarding service.
- www.smallanimalsboarding.co.uk: A British company that boards 30 different animals ranging from snakes and spiders to chinchillas and chipmunks.
- www.fabcats.org/catteries: Full of advice about boarding catteries.

CHAPTER 63

A CAR FULL OF ANIMALS

PET-TAXI SERVICE

A busy cat owner may not have time to go to the vet. A dog owner might need someone to pick up his pooch at the kennel. Moving a dog or cat from the home of one family member to that of another is another service some owners need. Your assignment, if you choose to accept it, is to be on call to take those animals wherever they need to go. Your reward is a fun business with plenty of furry friends.

When you are a chauffeur for animals, you can listen to whichever radio station you like—one advantage to driving animals versus humans. It's a venture that's easy and inexpensive to start, assuming you already have a car. It can also be simple compared to many businesses. No chauffeur's license is required to carry animals, and word-of-mouth marketing might be enough to get you started. It is even possible that yours will be the first pet taxi service in town.

Money

Rates vary in this relatively new business. Some of the pricing schemes you'll find with existing pet taxis are $15 per hour plus a fuel surcharge; $10 per ride plus $1 per mile; and $25 per hour with the first 10 miles free, plus $1 per mile after that. A minimum charge of $10 to $15 is common. The most frequent requests are for rides to and from animal hospitals and kennels, but long-distance relocation is sometimes needed, and trips to the airport are becoming more common.

Although some pet taxi companies focus just on rides for cats and dogs, which makes for a simpler business, for bigger profits you'll eventually want to offer other services to pet owners. This business works perfectly with pet-monitoring services (checking and feeding animals while the owners are out of town or too busy) and dog walking, for example. You might also offer grooming services once you learn the skills. Pet-service businesses with an employee or two often make more than $100,000 annually.

How to Get Started

A van is ideal, but any car can be used for this business. Buy a couple of cat carriers and a simple dog cage, since not every owner will have these items, and you don't want animals running under your feet when you're driving. You can buy harnesses for dogs, which leave them with more freedom to move but still keep them attached to safety belt clips. If the owners do have something they normally transport their pets in, using it not only saves you time washing your own equipment but also allows both dogs and cats to feel more comfortable in a carrier they are familiar with.

To market your business, you can start with magnetic signs for the sides of your car and some business cards. Some of the latter should be left with veterinarians, animal groomers, and anyone else who can refer customers to you. Certification of some sort, which can be obtained from one of the many animal-care-providers associations, will help you present yourself as a professional.

Resources

- www.petride.com: An example of a pet taxi service in New York City.
- www.petsitters.org: You can get certified as a pet sitter here, which may help with marketing.
- www.youtube.com: Search "pet taxi business" and you'll find several videos on starting a pet taxi business.

CHAPTER 64

SIT, FETCH, AND ROLL OVER

ANIMAL TRAINER

Teaching dogs to sit, to wait, and to fetch may be the most typical work that an animal trainer does, but possibilities abound beyond teaching simple obedience and tricks. Animals of all sorts need to be prepared for movies, for example, and marine parks need trainers for their dolphins and whales. Dogs need to be taught skills for security work, horses need to be readied for riding, and several species assist people with disabilities.

Patience and a desire to work with animals are necessary qualifications, but at this time working as a trainer rarely has legal requirements. Employers may have requirements, of course. For example, to work with whales at SeaWorld you'll probably need a bachelor's degree in biology, marine biology, or animal science. The most accessible animal-training jobs are at corporate pet store chains, and running obedience classes for dogs and cats is the most common position. Zoos, petting parks, and other places with animals also hire trainers to conduct educational programs.

Money

The Bureau of Labor Statistics shows the average annual wage of animal trainers as $31,080, but about 10 percent make more than $52,000. The 10,000 employees in this field work a variety of different jobs in reality, of course, and a dog trainer at a pet store is likely to make significantly less than that average, while a dolphin trainer at an amusement park can make much more. The BLS does not track business income, however, and running your own business as an animal trainer is where the most potential profit is.

How to Get Started

Even if you've already worked with animals for quite a while, training and/or certification will help you get hired or find customers for your services. If you have some experience with a particular type of animal, whether that means you've been riding horses for years or teaching cats to do tricks, this is a good place to start. If you have no real experience, the easiest positions to get hired into are in dog obedience training. Petco, for example, which hires dog trainers primarily from students of ABTA, a sister company of the Animal Behavioral College (see the resources section), has more than 600 stores that need trainers. From there you can work your way into other fields.

Starting your own animal-training company is an option at some point, and more feasible if you focus on dogs, cats, or horses. If you want to be a trainer of dolphins, elephants, or other less common animals, you'll have to plan ahead and work hard. It can take several years to get into these areas, even as an assistant to a trainer. Talk to someone in the position you would like to see what specific steps you'll need to take.

Resources

- *Animal Training: Successful Animal Management through Positive Reinforcement* by Ken Ramirez (Shedd Aquarium Society, 1999): Focuses on marine animal training.
- www.bigbendfarm.com: Trainers of border collies for goose control, which sell for $3,000 to $7,000.
- www.animalbehaviorcollege.com: A vocational school that teaches and certifies animal trainers at locations around the country. Check out the stories from real people working in the industry.
- www.animaltraining.org: Disney's animal-training-program web site, with stories and tips on training everything from squirrels to Komodo dragons.
- www.antlerdogs.com: An example of a small niche. This company trains dogs to find and retrieve antlers shed by deer and elk, and sells a video, too.

CHAPTER 65

CAGING WILD KITTENS

CAT ENCLOSURES

When we moved to our new home, the neighbor told us that three of his cats had been killed by coyotes. We also found out that indoor cats live, on average, three times as long as outdoor cats. Of course, our cats, Jack and Opie, wanted fresh air and to see birds without glass in between. The solution? An outdoor cat enclosure. Ours is an eight-by-eight-foot cage that the cats can enter from inside through a little door. Smaller designs are meant to be accessed through a window.

More and more people are realizing that a healthy cat needs a mentally stimulating environment, complete with fresh air. Outdoor enclosures accomplish that. Most of them are currently sold online as kits (see the resources section), but some fencers have begun doing enclosures and cat-proofing of whole yards. Top-end enclosures that are about six by eight feet go for $3,000 or more. Cat-proofing of yards costs more than normal fencing because it takes special materials. This is a great outdoor business if you like building things and working with cats.

Money

Building cat enclosures is a relatively new industry with little competition. Unable to find a local company, we built our own for $110 in materials and later saw similar ones online selling for around $2,000. When we found a fencer with some experience making animal enclosures, we had our whole backyard cat-proofed. Current competition is from companies selling kits through web sites and others selling cat-proofing fencing and related supplies. You can go that route, but based on the amount of interest our enclosure has generated, I suspect there is good demand for on-site building of rooms as well as cat-proofing of yards or existing fences.

Since this on-site-building part of the industry is so new, estimates of demand and potential profits are speculative, but I can assure you that many of us cat owners do not want to buy do-it-yourself kits. Don't limit your potential by pricing your service too low. You need prices that allow you to someday hire employees and still make a decent profit on each project. If you did a job every weekend with an average profit of $500, you would make $26,000 annually, part-time.

How to Get Started

If you have a cat of your own, build a cat enclosure for it. Better yet, make two for your cat, using different designs. Connect them with a cat tunnel, another product you can sell. Note how long it takes, how much the materials cost, and whether you enjoy the process. Take photos to start your portfolio. If you don't have a cat, build an enclosure for a friend. The experience will tell you if this business is right for you. You can find design ideas on many web sites by searching the terms "cat enclosures" and "catteries." Check with local authorities to see if building or fencing permits are needed (sometimes it depends on the size of the room you build).

Resources

- www.cagesbydesign.com: Click on the tab for cat cages and you'll see photos that will give you an idea of what is possible with cat enclosures.
- www.catsofaustralia.com/cat-enclosures.htm: This site has some photos of the smaller window-cages for cats.
- www.purrfectfence.com: Cat-fence-enclosure systems and components; a good supplier if you want to offer the service of cat-proofing yards.
- http://habitathaven.com: A cat enclosure company in Toronto; photos from installations in more than 40 Canadian and U.S. cities.

PART NINE

CREATIVE AND ARTISTIC WORK

Making walking sticks was the closest thing I've had to artistic work. I anchored glass balls in the tops of some sticks and inlaid rear-view mirrors in others. But soon, with a few basic designs and a systematic approach, I started producing walking sticks in less than 30 minutes each. The creative part just wasn't as important to me as getting my time investment down in order to get the profit per hour up. Writing, on the other hand, is more of a creative passion for me. Although I sometimes have to focus on efficiency, I return again and again to more creative efforts with my writing, both in fiction and nonfiction. We're at our most creative and artistic when we're inspired by the right kind of work.

Perhaps one of the jobs and businesses in this section will be the kind of work that motivates *you* and brings out *your* creative and artistic abilities. It could be using your voice to create characters or promote products. It might involve inventing new household gadgets or painting three-dimensional murals that cover whole sides of buildings. Or perhaps you are meant to carve walking sticks—but with more care and artistry than my own efforts demonstrated.

PHIL BLACK, INVENTOR OF FITDECK

Phil Black has been a personal trainer, firefighter, and Navy Seal—not the most likely background for an inventor. But his résumé also includes Yale University; Harvard Business School; and experience as an entrepreneur, author, and speaker. Obviously a man of diverse talents, in 2004 Black started FitDeck Inc. to sell a new product he invented for the physical wellness market. I asked him about the origin of his idea and how he made it into a marketable product.

What did you do for a living before you started FitDeck?
I was a bond trader for Goldman Sachs in New York City for two years before joining the navy. I attended Naval Officer Candidate School and became a naval

officer on my way to Navy SEAL training. I was a Navy SEAL officer for almost six years before leaving the navy to attend Harvard Business School. Upon graduation, I moved to San Diego to start FitDeck.

How did you come up with the idea for exercise playing cards, and exactly how are they used by the customer?

I came up with the idea to create FitDeck after combining the fun of a card game I used to play in college with the rigors of my Navy SEAL training. The premise is simple: Shuffle the cards and flip a card over. Whatever the card says to do, you do it. Instant workout with endless variation.

It helps to have a great idea, but implementation is everything. What was one of your biggest challenges in making this business work?

Funding is always a challenge when starting a business.

How long was it before you could pay yourself a livable income from your business?

It took several years before we felt comfortable paying ourselves any significant money. Most of the money gets reinvested into the company to fuel future growth.

I see that you are now offering customized decks with company logos. How important do you think continuing innovation is to the growth of a company like yours?

Extremely important. We will have a digital representation of all of our FitDeck titles available on smartphones, iPads, laptops, etc. in the coming months. Innovate or die.

Are most of your sales from your web site or through retailers?

Most of our sales currently are online, though our retail reach is beginning to take hold.

What have you really enjoyed about the whole process of inventing and marketing a new product, and which tasks have been the least enjoyable?

The creative side of the business is the most fun. To take things that come out of your own head and see them appear on a product that people actually buy and love—is quite gratifying. The least enjoyable aspect is probably the constant over-load of "to dos." There is never enough time to get to everything. It's hard to turn off and relax with so much to do.

Can you offer any other advice to those who are thinking about try-ing to invent and sell a new product?

Love the product or service. The road is long, arduous, and will make you doubt yourself over and over. If you don't love the idea or it's not in an area that you are an expert in, it will be hard to keep up the motivation and drive.

CHAPTER 66

BIRD-POOP EARRINGS

UNIQUE JEWELRY

Years ago, a small company collected the droppings from different species of birds, then encased them in acrylic and made them into earrings and necklaces. I don't know if it's still around, but at the time it was in the news because of its success. A few jewelry makers do sell bird-poop earrings online now, but it seems that fake poop is the norm. In any case, this example does show just how creative you can get with a handcrafted jewelry business.

Earrings, bracelets, and necklaces can be made from coins, bullets, animal bones, doll parts, nuts, bolts, and random found-objects. I recently saw a necklace made of a string of photos of eyes embedded in acrylic discs. I used to make bracelets out of woven cedar roots, although I never sold them. My wife and I did sell fish-scale earrings at flea markets and craft shows. They were handmade ones we brought back from a trip to Ecuador. If you like jewelry, and you think it sounds like fun to create your own unusual and unique designs, you might develop jewelry making into an extra income or perhaps even a large business.

Money

Gross profit margins are good with jewelry because materials rarely cost more than a fraction of the price. Unique pendants often sell for $50 to $150, and earrings for $15 to $75, and the materials to make them can be just a few dollars. You do have to invest in tools, but your profit per piece is largely a question of the expenses of selling. A common way to sell is on consignment in art galleries, jewelry stores, and other retail locations, for example, which can mean the store owner keeping as much as half of the price. Art shows can be better or worse. Have a sufficient supply of your best-sellers ready if you go this route. It's no fun to have your gross profit of $600 for the weekend eaten up by the space rental and hotel bill.

Other ways to sell include home jewelry parties, web sites, and wholesaling to retailers. Wholesaling works best with inexpensive, popular jewelry that you can make quickly—the latter being important because the biggest impediment to making much money is the limited amount of time you have to create. Starting your own store at a physical location, online, or both, and selling other artists' jewelry alongside yours can be much more profitable. Several handmade jewelry businesses in the United States top $1 million in annual sales.

How to Get Started

Play around with some ideas, buy a few basic tools and supplies, and start finding your creative niche. You can work at home and you'll probably never need a permanent retail location. Start a small web site, using a service like PayPal to process credit card payments, to keep your setup costs low. Add a few fliers or cards to that and you're in business for a few hundred dollars.

Resources

- *Jewelry Making and Beading For Dummies* by Heather Dismore and Tammy Powley (For Dummies, 2004): Written for do-it-yourselfers but full of ideas.
- *Marketing and Selling Your Handmade Jewelry: The Complete Guide to Turning Your Passion into Profit* by Viki Lareau (Interweave Press, 2006).
- www.parrotjewelry.com: An example of a woman who sells parrot-themed jewelry, including parrot poop designs.
- www.jewelrydelmundo.com: Artisan jewelry made with fish scales, bamboo, and many other materials.
- www.home-jewelry-business-success-tips.com: Information on making and selling your own jewelry.

CHAPTER 67

YOU'LL LIKE THE SOUND OF THIS

VOICE-OVER WORK

Are you ready to be a singing squirrel, a cartoon raccoon, or a talking tuna? Or maybe you can be the unseen announcer for the newest game show, or the narrator for a documentary. These are just some of the possibilities for voice-over actors. And although the big money is more often in Hollywood or New York City, you can find a way to get started in almost any part of the country. You might do radio commercials for local businesses, or be the announcer for television infomercials. You can do audiobook recordings at a local studio, even if you're hired by a company across the country. Narration for museum exhibit recordings or doing tapes for self-guided tours are other possible jobs.

Although you will generally need training, you do not need a college degree to get into this line of work. With a few voice lessons and a demo tape, you are ready to start looking for work where you live. Then, with that local experience, you can look for better-paying projects in larger cities. With hard work and a bit of luck, you could even gain fame and fortune as the voice of the next hottest cartoon character.

Money

The median wage for radio and television announcers in the United States is only $27,500, with about 10 percent of employees in the field making more than $76,000. Until you have a lot of experience, you're likely to make $15 to $20 per hour for small jobs, many of which will provide only a day or two of work. If you're most interested in voice acting for animated films or being the next unseen "Charlie" of *Charlie's Angels*, you might join the Screen Actors Guild. Even for minor roles you can expect to make $600 or more per day as a member of SAG, but you are not allowed to take nonunion jobs, which can mean passing up many opportunities to work. If you do decide to join, wait until you have experience.

How to Get Started

You'll need training to develop the quality and consistency of your voice and to determine what areas you'll do best in. You might have a deep voice that works well for radio commercials, or perhaps you have the ability to do 13 different cartoon voices. In addition to getting some help from a voice coach, you can volunteer to be the announcer for any events you might be involved with. Practice at home as well.

You may want to buy some high-quality sound equipment at some point, especially if you hope to work from home at times (doing audiobooks, for example). If you do not have your own equipment, you'll have to pay a local studio to prepare your demo tapes. You need at least a few minutes of voice-over spots. If necessary, just make them up. As long as they sound good, it is not crucial that they're real commercials you did. When you're ready, you will also need a good agent.

Resources

- *The Art of Voice Acting, Third edition: The Craft and Business of Performing for Voice-Over* by James Alburger (Focal Press, 2006).
- *There's Money Where Your Mouth Is: An Insider's Guide to a Career in Voice-Overs,* Second edition, by Elaine A. Clark (Back Stage Books, 2000).
- www.voices.com: Membership gets you access to job postings, and this company handles voice-over workers in more than 100 languages.
- www.edgestudio.com: A studio that also offers voice-over training.

CHAPTER 68

PAINT YOURSELF A PROFIT

MURAL-PAINTER

A multiple artist mural-painting event is planned for our little town here in Colorado, which will liven up many of the old buildings. It will also provide a marketing opportunity for the artists who participate. A lot of mural work is done indoors, but the outdoor work gets more attention, and so can bring new business to good painters. If that sounds like fun, and you have some experience creating art, painting murals can be a great way to make extra income or even earn a good living.

As a muralist your style might be realistic or cartoonlike. You may do traditional work or trompe l'oeil (murals that fool viewers into thinking they are actual scenes). You might limit your work to indoors or outdoors. You can specialize in scenery, abstract paintings, photo murals, or do just children's bedrooms. At some point you might choose or fall into a creative niche that is all yours.

Money

Prices vary, and the *way* prices are calculated varies. Some painters provide a rough estimate but charge $50 per hour. Others bid a job based on a variety of factors, with a minimum of $1,000 for any project. Charging per square foot is common. One how-to article suggests that beginning muralists charge $7 or less per square foot, but experienced painters get $20 to $80 per square foot. Typically, size is not the only factor. The amount of detail and type of paint matters too. Oil paint is more expensive than acrylic, for example. The charge for a simple mural covering part of a bedroom wall might be $1,200, while a large, detailed mural covering the side of a building can be tens of thousands of dollars. You're making art, of course, not just painting a wall, so prices will eventually be based on your creativity, skill, and reputation.

Growing your business can involve hiring employees at some point. The rewards can be worth it. One of the mural-painting companies I discovered in researching this chapter has about 10 employees and does more than $5 million in annual sales.

How to Get Started

Study the techniques others use, get some training, and start painting. You need a portfolio of your work to get jobs. To start, you may have to do a few free or cheap jobs for friends or perhaps for nonprofit organizations you would like to help out. Eventually you should have high-quality photos of six or more murals you have painted.

After you buy your basic supplies, you can get additional equipment as you need it. Bedroom walls can be done with a step stool, but you'll need to get a ladder or two if you get hired for a ceiling project. If you have the talent already, and you don't want to risk much time or money starting your own business, mural-painting companies that have several employees sometimes need more. You might work as an assistant at first, which is a good way to get experience.

Resources

- *How to Start a Faux Painting or Mural Business: A Guide to Making Money in the Decorative Arts* by Rebecca Pitman (Allworth Press, 2003).
- *Mural Painting Secrets for Success: Expert Advice for Hobbyists and Pros* by Gary Lord (North Light Books, 2008).
- www.findamuralist.com: Post a portfolio of your work here to get jobs, and check out the thousands of murals.
- www.thefauxschool.com: Mural-painting training.
- www.pawelbendiszart.com: An example of someone in the business.

CHAPTER 69

PUTTING ANTLERS ON DOGS

GADGETS AND GIFTS INVENTOR

Have you seen those silly reindeer antlers people put on their dogs and cats every Christmas? They've lasted a lot longer than the pet rock, and more than two million of them have been sold so far. Harvey Reese, the inventor, still gets royalties from every sale. Doesn't it sound fun to invent gadgets, gifts, and useful tools and get income from your creations for many years to come?

Making prototypes and marketing can be difficult, but ideas will come from all around you. Consider a simple example. I've been cutting pens down to three inches in length for 10 years so I can easily carry them in a pocket. Just last week I finally found a telescopic pen that can be put away short and opened up to normal length. I was happy to pay $5 for a set of two, and if an even shorter one is invented, I'll buy that. Make a quick list of things you wish existed or things that irritate you and others, and you have the inspiration necessary to solve problems by way of new products.

Money

Inventors' income is perhaps more variable than that of any other job or business covered in this book. Many creators will never make a dime despite having a hundred good ideas. Inventions don't sell themselves, and failure to learn marketing or to get help with it is why most inventors make very little money.

Potential profits are just a guess then, but examples abound. Consider Foot Petals. Tina Aldatz-Norris stepped on hot coals from a fire on the beach, burning her feet, which often blistered after that. She thought existing food pads and gels were ugly, so in 2001 she invented Foot Petals, which are self-adhesive pads shaped like flowers. Stick them inside your shoes and you have an attractive way to comfort your feet. Aldatz-Norris did $9 million in sales in 2007, for a net profit of $1.9 million. And at two million sales and counting,

Harvey Reese says he still gets 21 cents for each set of dog reindeer antlers sold. He has licensed 100 products over the years.

How to Get Started

Get the e-book *How to Have New Ideas* at my web site 999ideas.com. It's free, as is the use of any ideas on the site. But keep in mind that ideas make no money without implementation. If you really want to make your inventions pay, you have to learn all about the process and especially the marketing. Start with good books that use true stories to demonstrate how people have succeeded with new products. Also, when the time comes, seriously consider licensing your invention to a company that knows how to sell things, to avoid the risk of investing a lot of your own money in your own marketing efforts. With a good nondisclosure contract, you can present your idea to potential licensees prior to obtaining a patent, which can keep your costs down.

Resources

- *The Big Idea: How to Make Your Entrepreneurial Dreams Come True* by Donny Deutsch and Catherine Whitney (Hyperion, 2008).
- *Inventing For Dummies* by Pamela Riddle Bird (For Dummies, 2004).
- *Inventor's Notebook: A Patent It Yourself Companion* by Fred E. Grissom and David Pressman Attorney (NOLO, 2008).
- www.money4ideas.com: An invention-licensing company I've used and recommend. Click through to the inventors tips section, too.
- www.fitdeck.com: An example of a recent invention that is making money for the inventor.

CHAPTER 70

A BURNING DESIRE TO CREATE?

AROMATHERAPY-CANDLE MAKER

You can help people invigorate their minds with peppermint, eucalyptus, and rosemary scents. Or they can light up one of your jasmine candles as a stress reducer and aphrodisiac (the latter benefit might be the better marketing angle). Making and selling specialty candles is fun, has low setup costs, and can be done at home. And many low-competition niches exist beyond aromatherapy. You can make outrageously shaped candles, for example. I have seen them in the shape of a hand, with a wick coming out of each finger, and there are dynamite, beer mug, and cactus-shaped ones too. One company does only uncommon scents like whiskey, coffee, pizza, and cotton candy.

In addition to choosing your niche in candles, you can choose how to sell them. Some people like to sell their creations at craft shows. Others wholesale them to gift stores and various retailers. If you like to stay home, you can sell exclusively from a web site. Or you can do all three of these.

Money

Prices are based on size and uniqueness. The scent can be a factor if essential oils are used because some (like jasmine) will cost you much more than others. Artistic candles typically sell for $20 to $40 each. Small novelty ones (shaped like cacti, for example) might sell for a few dollars each or in sets. A single aromatherapy candle in a jar or can (easy to make) will typically sell for $10 to $20. The web site WelcomeHome-Candles.com currently has a luxury candle (gold-and-diamond trimmed) for $4,995.

Making high-end high-margin candles might not be a bad strategy for your business (you don't have to sell nearly so many to make a decent income). In addition to approaching stores to sell your candles, and setting up a web site to sell them directly, you might someday sell your own and others' artistic creations in your own candle store. For example, the Candle Factory has thrived in little Traverse City, Michigan (population 15,000), for 40 years. How much can you make with candles? Search "candle manufacturers" at Manta.com and you'll find 200 that top $1 million in revenue. Even a search of "candle makers" (generally these are the craft businesses) yields a couple of businesses at that level.

How to Get Started

You need molds, wicks, dyes, scents, and a pan to melt the wax. A few hundred dollars in materials and you're ready. To keep costs low, you can rely on word-of-mouth advertising at first, and then invest your profits back into marketing your business to grow it. The start-up costs are less with paraffin, but many customers like the idea of natural beeswax candles, and you can sell them for more. You might start cheap and upgrade later, but it is probably better to start defining your niche from the start, including which materials you'll use. You can sell your candles at an online craft marketplace like Etsy .com until you're ready to have your own web site.

Resources

- *Candlemaking for Fun and Profit* by Michelle Espino (Potter Craft, 2000): Covers basic candle making for fun and doing it as a home business.
- www.hotwicks.com: An example of an unusual candle business, with bacon-, beer-, and grass-scented candles.
- www.candlebusinesscorner.com: This site calls itself "The Candle Making Business Resource." Articles, marketing plans, and business forms are free.
- www.fragrantpassagecandleco.com: Sellers of wholesale candles.
- www.candles.net: A candle store that has done well for many years in a small town in Michigan.

CHAPTER 71

CARVING OUT A NICHE

WALKING STICKS

While hiking one day, I noticed hundreds of young, straight, white cedar trees in a swamp. Most had recently died, as is common when they grow too thick. I cut one and made a walking stick, then cut more. Later I spent two hours in a thicket of young poplar trees and returned to my van with 50 of them. By the end of that summer, I had made and sold hundreds of walking sticks. Some had glass beads inset on top; others were inlaid with tiny rear-view mirrors. I cut leather from thrift-store jackets into strips to make handgrips. With less than a dollar in each for materials, my primary investment was time.

Carving and selling walking sticks is a great way to express your creativity and to make money, but more the former than the latter, unless you find the right niche. Special designs, unique woods, and artistic flair are what you need. It's a business you can start for the price of a pocketknife and do at home, working when you like.

Money

If you're talented enough, target the high end of this market to get $80 or more per walking stick. Expensive ones sell best at arts and crafts shows. Mine, not that artistic, sold for $10 to $24 each, and on my best day I made only $200. I also wholesaled dozens at a time to vendors who worked gun shows and pow-wows. Some carvers sell them online for as low as $30 now, but most are in the $50 to $90 range.

The more unique your creations, the less direct competition you'll have. Sticks with spiral snake carvings are currently selling online for $250 each. Special woods are worth more too. Make one from a muscle-wood tree (they look like sinewy muscles) and your buyer will have the only one his friends have seen. You can charge more for inlaid gems, pewter figurines (glue and nail them into the stick), or carved animal heads. This is a low-overhead business, even with a web site. Work weekends, sell six sticks weekly for a gross profit of $60 each, and you'll have an extra income of about $18,000 per year. To do much more you need to produce them quickly (I took less than an hour each) and wholesale large batches. You can also buy other carvers' sticks and sell them, in which case, making $20 each and selling a dozen daily from a web site would produce a gross profit of over $87,000 annually.

How to Get Started

Experiment to see what you're best at. Check with public land authorities about cutting in national forests, or get permission from landowners who need their trees thinned. You can also make walking sticks out of purchased wood, like the bamboo gardening centers sell (buy the one-inch pieces). A knife and small saw to cut trees are all you need to start, although you may want to buy other tools depending on the designs you choose to make. A Dremel rotary tool is great for detailed carvings of animals.

Resources

- *Make Your Own Walking Sticks: How to Craft Canes and Staffs from Rustic to Fancy* by Charles Self (Fox Chapel Publishing, 2007): Detailed instructions for some great designs.
- www.coloradowalkingsticks.com: Dick Bryant makes and sells some really nice walking sticks.
- www.whistlecreek.com: An example of a company that sells sticks made by others, and supplies for stick makers.

CHAPTER 72

PROFITS FROM PAINTING PEOPLE

TEMPORARY TATTOOS

You've probably seen kids getting temporary tattoos at festivals and other events. Maybe you have even paid for your own kids to get a fish or a sun or other design put on their skin. Many adults would also like a tattoo but don't like the irreversibility of traditional ones. Something that lasts a few days is ideal. As a provider of this service, you can focus your marketing on an age-based or social group, or you can aim to provide unique body art for anyone who wants it.

The two most common types of temporary tattoos are stick-on ones and those done with an airbrush. The first can be applied more quickly and cheaply, making them perfect for a crowded festival full of families, where you want to serve as many customers as you can in a few short hours. Airbrushing produces a higher-quality job, and if you are really skilled and artistic you can work freehand in addition to using the usual stencils.

Money

With stick-on tattoos costing as little as 7 cents and airbrushed ones generally less than a dollar in materials, this a high-margin business. You'll get a few dollars each for applying stick-ons and $5 to $30 for airbrushed ones. For airbrush tattoos you normally use stencils, but if you *can* eventually do them freehand, try to charge more for your unique artistry.

You'll typically set up a stand at festivals, craft shows, graduation parties, birthday parties, church events, street markets, Halloween parties, and in high tourist-traffic locations. One seller of turnkey airbrush systems claims that some of their clients have done $60,000 the first year in business. Based on their own and clients' experience, they project sales of $1,000 to $1,500 daily for street festivals with 50,000 people, $2,000 for amusement parks with 5,000 people attending, and $5,000 monthly for beauty and tanning salons.

Efficiency is important. I've seen lines at festival tattoo booths many times, suggesting that how much money the vendor made for the day was largely dependent on how fast the customers were seated, painted, and collected from. Try a few different setups, always have enough change, and practice the whole routine until you can do it quickly without your clients feeling rushed. A realistic goal, assuming you pay $100 for a spot at a busy festival and charge $10 per tattoo (average), is 80 airbrushed tattoos for a net profit of about $650 for the day.

How to Get Started

The least expensive way to get started is with the stick-on tattoos. Airbrushing makes more money, though, so it can be worth the higher setup cost. You'll need an airbrush, a compressor (get the silent studio type), paints, and stencils. It's also a good idea to have rubbing alcohol and baby oil with you at all times to remove tattoos or to correct mistakes (they won't wash off with soap and water). Although you might save a few hundred dollars buying everything separately, it's much easier to start with a complete system. These typically cost $3,000 to $4,000 and come with telephone and e-mail support—a big advantage of starting this way.

Resources

- www.europeanbodyart.com: Airbrush tattoo systems and supplies, and support for those starting businesses.
- www.airbrush-tattoos.com: An example of a family-oriented temporary tattoo business.
- http://youtube.com: Search "temporary tattoos" and you'll find many good video tutorials to get you started.
- www.bodygraphics.ca: Inexpensive franchise packages for stick-on tattoo businesses.
- www.tattoosales.com: Bulk sellers of stick-on tattoos.

PART TEN

BUYING AND SELLING THINGS

At 11 years old, I bought hard candy in bags to get the cost per piece down, and then sold the candy individually in school, for a 100 percent markup. Because it was against school rules, I carried my inventory in a book I had hollowed out and in hidden pockets I had sewn on the inside of my jacket. I also bought and sold old coins and comic books. Later in life, when I had my first home, I put a grocery store in the closet to make more money from the tenants I rented rooms to. The simplicity of buying something at the best price you can get and then selling it for a higher price is very appealing.

What can you buy and sell? You'll find a few ideas that are often overlooked in this section, including an entry explaining how some people are running dollar stores without a store or overhead. Rack merchandising is another business you might not have thought of. And did you know there are big profits to be had selling buckets of nitrogen-packed wheat and other supplies to survivalists? Or perhaps you'll have more fun as a liquidation broker.

RUSTY AND DEBBIE LAKE, CLASSIC FURNITURE

After years of living overseas, Rusty and Debbie Lake came back to the United States and needed a way to make a living, so they started Classic Furniture in Cañon City, Colorado. In their store, they sell quality preowned furniture on consignment, buy and sell some items outright, and also carry new items occasionally. My wife and I have been customers on both sides of the equation, buying things and selling things in their store numerous times. I've often wondered about the nature of their business, so I was happy to be able to ask Rusty a few questions.

How (and why) did you get into the secondhand furniture business?

We had lived out of the United States for many years and were looking for a viable business upon our return. After some research and input from friends who had a similar business in Salida, we decided that Cañon City was a good market for the business.

You operate in a small town, but apparently it is big enough. How large would you guess a town needs to be to support a furniture business like yours?

Cañon City is almost too small for a reasonable income for this type of business. We have added a moving company to our business to enable us to make an income that is adequate. Larger cities definitely provide a better income for this type of business.

Was your business hurt by the recession, or do sales of used items go up during tough times?

Our business has been active for three and a half years, but much of that time the economy has been in recession. Our business has grown during the recession. This may be because good furniture is available for a reasonable price but also because people are becoming more aware of our product.

Knowing what you now know, if you had to start the business over, is there anything you would you do differently?

We did not anticipate our need for vehicles, and we did not adequately predict our overhead costs.

One advantage of selling consignment furniture is that you don't need as much capital to get started, since you don't pay up front for inventory. But you still need basic tools, and you need to rent a place to do business. If a person already has a pickup truck and lives in a town with enough demand, do you think he or she could start a business like yours for a few thousand dollars?

If one wants to make a reasonable profit, it requires a large trailer and preferably a small truck. We find our profit is significantly more with furniture we buy as opposed to the 40 percent we receive from sales of consignments. There needs to be a sizable volume of sales to make a reasonable profit. We are fortunate to live in a town with low-cost retail property for rent. Overhead in many places is much more than we have. High volume is necessary for a reasonable profit.

After years of doing this, you must have learned quite a bit. What advice would you offer someone who wanted to start a consignment furniture shop in his own town?

I would advise people to stay out of debt. If at all possible do not rely on this business as a sole source of income in the beginning. It takes time to develop loyal customers and a good reputation. The most important thing is to develop a strong customer base through personal relationships and service that is high above the norm. If one exercises reasonably good business practices, learns his market, and truly cares about the customers served, the business will prosper.

CHAPTER 73

I SEE DEAD PEOPLE PROFITS

ESTATE GOODS

When people die, their families are left with all the accumulated possessions of a lifetime. They usually have no interest in trying to find the right buyer to get the most out of each item, so they simply hire an auction service to run an estate sale. The result is that everything goes, and as often as not, some things go cheaply—very cheaply.

Making money from the leftovers of estates involves buying items that can be sold for a profit. A rummage sale is sometimes held followed by an auction. You can find profitable opportunities at either of these. Once you know the business well, you can even approach families to buy the entire contents of the home of the deceased. Where do you sell what you find? It is often best to sell furniture locally, while items that are easier to ship can be sold online to get the highest price.

Money

If you search eBay for sellers of used items (which could be purchased from any number of sources, including estate sales), you'll find many who have sold *thousands* of items. Assuming they make a profit on each sale, the potential here is obvious. More exact figures are difficult to come by, since this is not a traditional type of business for which there is data from government or other sources. An example of a successful store that relies on estate sales for inventory can be found in the resources section.

You can advertise furniture and large items on Craigslist.com for local sales. You can also place these things with consignment stores, or sell outright to used furniture stores if you buy items cheaply enough. To sell online through eBay and other auction sites, buy with a $10 minimum profit in mind, or you'll invest too much time for the money. If you have any eBay trading assistants near you, you can have them handle selling and shipping for you. If you buy and sell 58 items weekly, with an average gross profit of $30 each, and have $10,000 in costs, you would net about $80,000 for the year. Another option is to become an estate liquidator. A handful of these companies top $1 million in annual sales.

How to Get Started

This is a business that can be started with very little money and done from home. Attend a few estate sales. Take notes on numerous items and their asking prices as well as sales prices at the auctions. Look up identical or similar things for sale on eBay.com or Craigslist.com, to get an idea of where there might be a profit. As soon as you have educated yourself a bit on prices, buy a few things and sell them. You can grow your business from that start. If you come to know a niche really well, like lamps or jewelry, for example, you might find it more efficient and less risky to specialize.

Resources

- *Estate Sale Prospecting for Fun and Profit with Craigslist and eBay* by John Landahl (InfoStrategist.com, 2006).
- www.auctionzip.com: Listings of auctioneers in every state. Call ones near you to find out about coming estate auctions.
- www.ehow.com/how_4498593_money-ebay-estate-sale-items.html: An article explaining the basics of finding profitable items at estate sales.
- http://therustydime.net: An example of an antiques and collectibles business that is stocked largely from estate auctions.
- http://ebaytradingassistant.com: Search for an eBay specialist near you if you don't want to handle the selling yourself.

CHAPTER 74

THEIR LOSS IS YOUR GAIN

STORAGE UNIT AUCTIONER

A neighbor has a pop machine in his house, which he picked up at an auction. He bid on and bought the contents of a storage unit for $200, and the machine was one of the things included. It was new in the box, and probably could have been quickly sold for $600, making it a good example of the profit potential in these auctions.

People rent self-storage units to stash all the items that don't fit in their homes. When they don't pay the rent—perhaps because their money is going toward credit card debts accumulated from buying so much in the first place—the operator of the storage facility auctions off the contents of their units. Some facilities price and sell contents like a rummage sale. Others auction items off piece by piece. Most, however, keep it simple and auction the entire contents of each delinquent unit all at once. If you buy the contents cheaply, and sell a few of the items discovered for a decent price, you have a profit. Do this consistently and you have a business.

Money

Efficiency matters. It should be possible to attend several sales in a day. According to StorageAuctions.com, there are more than 2,900 self-storage facilities in California alone, and in any given month more than 800 of these have auctions. Take notes to determine where the best auctions are. The various facilities attract different clientele and therefore have different types of contents. Most of the time the highest bid is less than $300 for a unit.

On the sales end, you need to determine where you'll get the highest prices for various types of goods. Furniture will usually be sold locally, for example, while collectibles will get a better price on eBay. If you net $150 per unit and buy the contents of four of them every weekend, that adds up to over $31,000 annually, which is a nice part-time income that can grow into much bigger profits in time.

How to Get Started

This can be a difficult way to make much money until you learn where the best sales are and which items yield the most profit. On the other hand, it is easy to get into this business. A safe strategy to start with is to identify one or two items you know the value of, and bid no more than that for the whole lot. The known-value items will cover your cost when you sell them, and anything else of value becomes your profit. After a few sales you'll get better at determining how much to bid and which auctions are best.

Call local storage facilities to ask about upcoming auctions. They're also advertised in local newspapers. Some allow you to thoroughly pick through the contents of each unit, while others allow only a quick look. Some bidders specialize, looking for units full of books (which they often sell through Amazon.com), for example, or for furniture to supply a used furniture store. This makes sense if you know a lot about a particular type of goods. Fortunately, the managers of the facilities often advertise if there are musical instruments, book collections, or other specific categories of things.

Resources

- www.storageauctionsecrets.com: Information on making money with storage unit auctions on the site and in the e-book *Storage Auction Secrets*.
- www.storageauctions.com/3.htm: The web site of California Storage Auctions and News, with articles on storage auctions that are relevant beyond California.
- www.backwoodshome.com/articles2/wilson83.html: A good article from *Backwoods Home Magazine*.

CHAPTER 75

THE MIDDLEMAN ALWAYS GETS HIS CUT

LIQUIDATION BROKER

An acquaintance stumbled upon the opportunity to buy thousands of wooden clocks for pennies on the dollar, from a local factory that had closed a few years earlier. His idea was to sell them on eBay for a profit of perhaps $5 each. Although this isn't a bad way to make some money, my first thought was, "Couldn't you sell the whole batch to a chain of retail stores and make just a dollar each?" That would still be thousands in profit and a lot easier and faster. Obviously I'm more inclined toward wholesale than retail sales. If you are, too, being a closeout or liquidation broker might be the right business for you.

It starts as a treasure hunt, in which you look for stores that have unsold items they need to dump, or small manufacturers that have discontinued inventory. Shops that have gone out of business are another possible source of goods. You might find lamps, toys, jewelry, clothing, housewares, office supplies, electronics, and more. You buy cheap and then sell cheap in large lots to stores, liquidation retailers, flea market vendors, dollar stores, and other clients.

Money

The best way to understand the mechanics and profit potential of this business is with an example. Suppose you notice a toy store that is going out of business. Talking to the owner you find that even after a big closeout sale he'll likely have leftover inventory worth $100,000 retail by his final day. You find a small supermarket chain that will buy everything for $16,000, and you offer the owner $12,000. If he accepts your offer, you net perhaps $3,000 after the expense of shipping the toys to the stores.

183

Notice that if you arrange the deal before you buy, you have no risk. On the other hand, if you can't find a buyer, you might put up you own cash, offering $7,000 for the lot. Then you could sell batches over time for 12 percent of retail to flea market vendors, who will sell the toys for 25 percent of the normal store price. If you judge the market correctly and sell it all, you'll gross $5,000 on the toys. Find a deal like that twice monthly and you'll have gross profits of $120,000 annually. Searching merchandise liquidation companies (includes both brokers and retailers) at Manta.com produces several dozen companies that do $1 million or more in annual sales.

How to Get Started

You can start with small deals using your own cash, to get a feel for the process. For example, a retiree I know has 65 handmade birdhouses in his garage and may decide he's too old to do more craft shows. If he sold you his remainders for $300 ($4.61 each), and you drove around to gift shops until you wholesaled them all for $13 each (they'll retail for $30), you would make $545 for your effort. It might take only a day. Watch for stores closing in your area to find larger deals, and put your profits back into growing your business. Stick to brokering and wholesaling and you don't need to collect sales tax or deal with as much paperwork.

Resources

- www.tdwcloseouts.com/opportunities.html: Setup help, support, and web site hosting for closeout brokers.
- http://sdetech.com: An example of a liquidation broker.
- www.nationalwholesaleliquidators.com: Retailer of liquidated and closeout merchandise; a potential customer for a broker.
- www.closeoutcentral.com: Closeout deals are posted here.
- http://thecloseoutindustry.com: Click on "Closeout Education" for helpful articles.

CHAPTER 76

BARBER CHAIRS AND OTHER OPPORTUNITIES

USED AND UNUSUAL FURNITURE SELLER

I knew a woman who sold lamps on eBay and made a living at it. She primarily dealt in antiques and odd light fixtures, and did it all from home. Of course, furnishings like lamps are relatively easy to ship and so are more practical for online sales. You'll want your own retail location for larger furniture. Fortunately, even a storefront operation can be started with just a few thousand dollars if you make yours a consignment store.

To avoid competition, and to keep it simpler, you might specialize in one of the many possible niches. Some used furniture sellers handle only outdoor furniture. Others specialize in used barber chairs. You might market just items for children, or only those things made primarily of wood (you avoid cleaning fabrics on chairs and couches). You could even transform used tables into colorful and artistic pieces. You can get creative in many ways with used furniture.

Money

Properly setting up and stocking a used furniture store can cost $80,000. You can cut that to $10,000 if you make it a consignment store to avoid inventory costs. Another alternative is to try a niche that allows you to initially operate from a large garage at home. For example, restaurants and bars come and go, and some start with used tables or booths to reduce their initial investment. That makes for a nice niche. You might buy 20 used tables and 80 chairs from a bankrupt restaurant for $1,200, store them in your garage, carry samples in your truck or van to show potential buyers (owners of soon-to-open cafes, for example), and get $65 each for the tables and $20 for the chairs within a week, for a gross profit of $1,700. Parlay that into more deals and you'll soon have the capital to rent space for expansion.

The ultimate profit potential? Recent statistics on revenue of used furniture stores show several dozen that do better than $2 million annually. I just read a news story about two brothers who built a used office furniture business to $10 million in annual sales in two years, and without financing.

How to Get Started

To start a fully stocked specialty used furniture store, research the market and the going rental rates for retail space. Prepare a business plan even if you are fully funding the venture yourself, and include a calculation of your sales break-even point, based on all overhead costs and debt service payments. If it still looks feasible, go for it, but be sure to have some cash saved to carry you through. Retail businesses can lose money for many months before turning their first profit.

If you're short on capital and want a lower-risk start, you can buy used items at yard sales and thrift stores and resell them by advertising on Craiglist .com. Or you can focus on smaller items that can be easily shipped, and sell them on eBay. We have seen $20 items at rummage sales that would sell for $80 at our local consignment store, leaving a decent profit margin even after their 40 percent commission. Any of these strategies makes it possible to start with $100 and grow your business from the profits.

Resources

- www.entrepreneur.com/businessideas/827.html: An article on how to start a used furniture business.
- www.used-billiardtable.com: Used pool tables.
- http://barbertouch.com: Used barber chairs.
- www.officeliquidators.com: A company that does millions of dollars in annual sales focusing on used office furniture.

CHAPTER 77

FINDING NEW OWNERS
FOR OLD SHIRTS

USED CLOTHING SELLER

A pair of old jeans for $250? Years ago, during our brief stint as flea market vendors, my wife and I met a man who said he bought a pair of vintage Levis at a garage sale for 25 cents and had just sold them on eBay for $250. Skeptical, I went online that evening to see what old jeans sold for. At least 10 pairs had bids over $200. The bidding is less heated today, but I just saw an auction with a bid of $152 for vintage Levi's 501 jeans. There are 4,600 listings under "vintage jeans."

That is just one niche. Other specialties in used clothing include women's clothing, children's, vintage dresses, leather jackets, clothing worn by famous people, highest-quality items, name brands, and more. You also have many options for how to sell, including a store, a web site, selling on auction web sites, selling other people's clothing on consignment, and putting your own inventory in consignment shops. As with any business that involves used items, this is in part a treasure hunt. You can find your clothes at rummage sales, closeouts, thrift stores, and sale racks. The gentleman with the $200 jeans said he was even able to buy poorly marketed items cheap on eBay (people put things in wrong categories and so get low bids) and turn a profit reselling them on eBay with proper presentation.

Money

A big part of the profit potential is in how cheaply and how efficiently you buy your clothing. You can't make much buying baseball caps for 50 cents and selling them for $4 if it takes you all day searching rummage sales to find six of them. If you did choose to specialize in baseball caps, you would have to buy them 12 at a time at every thrift store nearby. Rummage sales, on the other hand, might be a good source for high-dollar vintage clothing, since a few finds daily could net you $1,000 per week.

If you open a consignment store to sell clothing for others, you'll typically keep half of every sale. You'll need a system for tracking sales and getting your consignees paid. Although stocking your store with your own inventory can mean a bigger initial investment, it is a simpler operation, and provided you find enough good clothing to fill the racks it can be more profitable. So is there really much money to be made in this industry? At Manta.com, you can search "used clothing," set the criteria at $500,000 in annual sales or higher, and you'll find hundreds of listings.

How to Get Started

For a creative business with little competition and little risk, try a small niche. For example, you might cherry-pick the 200 best T-shirts from the 50-cent racks at several thrift stores, then pay $15 for a spot at a flea market, where you're "The T-Shirt Man," selling them for $3 each. Your break-even point would be around 40 shirts, and if you sold 100 more you would be up $300 for the day. You could also start with one leather jacket at a time on eBay, and grow your business once you have experience and some profits to reinvest.

Resources

- www.estatefurs.com: An example of a used fur coat business.
- www.wornbutnotforgotten.com: Sellers of used children's clothing.
- www.cowboyway.com/FeltCowboyHats.htm: Sellers of used cowboy hats.
- www.ebay.com: Even if you don't want to sell on eBay, it is a great place to get educated on prices of various items.

CHAPTER 78

ONE MAN'S TRASH

ANTIQUE TREASURE HUNTER

The days when you needed $50,000 or more to become an antiques dealer are over. You can simply buy a classic old lamp at a yard sale for $15, sell it on eBay for $60, and you're in business. Put that profit into the next item or two, and repeat the process. At some point you might even build the capital to start a store if that's what you want. And when starting simply like this, you have no legal requirements other than getting a sales tax license if you sell to customers in your own state.

You can be a generalist, keeping your price guides handy as you hunt down the bargains, or you can specialize and become an expert in one of the many niches so you know a valuable find as soon as you see it. Some dealers focus on antique knives, guns, furniture, machines, or toys. You might even find a profitable niche in old collectibles like dolls or magazines. Other possibilities include porcelain, paintings and frames, stoneware, early glassware, tools, and country furniture.

Money

Antique dealers who make a full-time living from their business say that for a storefront operation you need to sell your items for three to six times what you pay. Large markups are necessary for you to have a decent profit after overhead and occasional losses and because you might have capital tied up for years in unsold inventory. Selling online you might do okay aiming to only double or triple your money on each purchase. If you choose to do business online it is perhaps best to concentrate on small collectibles that ship easily. Old fountain pens, for example, currently sell for between $100 and $1,000, and a 1953 Playboy magazine with Marilyn Monroe on the cover can fetch between $1,000 and $6,000. You might still sell the occasional large item, like a classic rolltop desk or wagon wheel, locally, by advertising on Craigslist.com.

Perhaps the most profitable approach is to have a store *and* sell online. You can use auction sites like eBay to quickly unload inventory that isn't moving so you can get that money invested in items that will move faster. Searching a business database I found 29,000 antique dealers in the United States. To narrow down that list to 100 or so, I had to set the criteria at $5 million or more in annual sales. There is a lot of money in antiques.

How to Get Started

Look for intriguing old things at thrift stores, rummage sales, and flea markets, and take a dozen photos. Then look on eBay to see what identical or similar items are selling for. Once you have the opportunity, buy something you can at least double your money with, and sell it. This will help you get familiar with the process, and help you determine if you like this kind of work. After that initial sale you can start studying the market, buying price guides, and looking at possible niches if you want to specialize. When you have more confidence, you can attend estate sales and auctions to load up on inventory.

Resources

- *How to Sell Antiques and Collectibles on eBay . . . And Make a Fortune!* by Dennis L. Prince (McGraw-Hill, 2004).
- *Warman's Antiques and Collectibles 2011 Price Guide*, 44th edition, by Mark F. Moran (Krause Publications, 2010).
- www.antique-knives.co.uk: Specialist in antique knives.
- www.antiqueslotmachines.com: A business based on antique slot machines.
- www.journalofantiques.com: A good place to start getting educated.

CHAPTER 79

A LITTLE HERE AND A LITTLE THERE

RACK MERCHANDISER

As a young man I invested $2,700 in earrings and display racks—a lot of money when you're making $3.40 per hour. The idea was to place racks in stores, beauty salons, and other locations and collect $3.50 for each $5-pair sold. The retailers got $1.50 per pair, and I made almost $2 after the cost of the jewelry. If I eventually placed 30 racks and they sold 15 pairs per week on average, I would have a gross profit of about $900 each week. That plan—even if it didn't quite work the way I hoped—describes the essence of rack merchandising. You put displays of greeting cards, toys, novelties, jewelry, candy, or any of a thousand other possibilities, in retail locations on consignment and run the route weekly to collect your profits and restock the racks. Consignees get *their* profits without investing in merchandise, which will often make it easier to sell them on the plan.

Wagon jobbing is similar, but you sell your products outright. For example, I once bought digital watches for 69 cents each, put them on nice displays, and sold them to retailers in batches of 20 for $30 total. They then sold them for $3 each. There are thousands of small point-of-purchase items (things sold near the cash register) that can help store owners boost profits while doing the same for you.

Money

The goal with rack merchandising is an easy route made up of locations that each net you a reasonable profit. For example, if you found a supply of country music CDs for $1 each, you might buy 100 racks that hold 50 CDs each, and get them placed in gas stations, convenience stores, and other locations within a 20-mile radius. If they sell for $5 and the retailer gets $2, you would also get $2 gross profit per sale. Average 10 sales weekly per rack and you have a gross profit of $104,000 annually. You might run the route every two weeks over the course of three days, restocking the racks and billing the stores $3 for each empty slot. With wagon jobbing you develop relationships with retailers who (you hope) trust you to bring them things that will sell. Some rack merchandising companies and wagon jobbers make millions annually. To avoid heavy competition and make this a more creative business, you might even invent your own product to sell.

How to Get Started

Rather than investing $5,000 in racks and inventory up front, start with investing six or seven different items in similar locations and watch to see which sell best. Then you can invest more into those products, and find additional locations. Sell things that you have a steady supply of for more predictable sales and easy restocking. If you buy closeouts and discontinued items, you'll have constantly changing products that may not sell equally well. It is better to sell these outright to store owners, and because they're often available for pennies on the dollar, you'll have good profit margins. You might experiment with both wagon jobbing like this and rack merchandising, to see where you do best.

Resources

- *Opportunities in Wagon Jobbing and Rack Merchandising—Special Report* by Dana Carter (Business eBook Reports, 2009): An Amazon Kindle e-book; you can download a free Kindle reader for your computer at Amazon.com.
- www.howtoadvice.com/WagonJobbing: Some information on rack merchandising and wagon jobbing.
- www.thebulletpoint.com/merchandising.html: My own true story about rack merchandising.
- www.dollaritem.com: Wholesale merchandise.

CHAPTER 80

A STORE WITH NO OVERHEAD

FLEA-MARKET DOLLAR STORE

When we lived in in Tucson, Arizona, we occasionally visited the Tanque Verde Swap Meet on weekends. With room for 400 vendors, and most spots filled, we always had a lot to look at. When we were in the business in Michigan, we heard many vendors say that it was more difficult than ever to make money. Since some of those at Tanque Verde had been there every weekend for 10 years, flea-market vending clearly still works for some, at least in the larger venues and special niches.

One particular type of business was clearly succeeding at flea markets we visited from Michigan to Arizona. I call it the flea-market dollar store. Companies doing this usually have at least one large panel truck, and in it they have 100 or more boxes or plastic tubs with goods. They arrange them in lines on the grass, with one row perhaps selling items that cost $5, another with $3 items, and several with $1 items. Those latter rows have many of the same things you see in every dollar store. This is a simple business with no overhead (everything can be stored in your garage), and it is perhaps the best way to make money with flea-market vending.

Money

I've been to flea markets with more than one successful dollar-store setup, but ideally you'll want to find markets that are busy and don't yet have this type of vendor. It is important to make your display neat and with prices clearly marked on each tub of goods. Customers will walk away if it's an effort to find the price of an item.

Buying cheap is obviously important, and you can find many wholesale merchandise outfits online now. As I write this, one has 6-cent toothbrushes; 3-cent postcards; kitchen utensils for 15 cents; and ashtrays, lipstick, and for-sale signs ranging from 37 to 47 cents. Fleece blankets can be bought in bulk for $2.76. It's difficult to find data on the revenue made from this, but I've seen vendors do thousands of dollars in sales per day, and with markups of 100 percent or more being typical, this suggests some great profit potential. One company that is actually called Flea Market Dollar Store, has an estimated annual revenue of $1 million and employs about 20 people, according to the business-data web site Manta.com.

How to Get Started

You'll need at least 60 tubs to start properly. Plastic ones with lids ($4 to $10 each) stack nicely and keep your inventory protected. Watch what people buy at dollar stores to get an idea of what to put in each tub, and order around twice the inventory you need to be fully stocked. Get a sales tax license, and find appropriate flea markets. Spaces typically run from $10 to $20 daily, but you'll need at least two adjacent ones, since they are usually small. Pay close attention to what sells well and you should be able to boost sales over time with better inventory.

If you first want a taste of the selling atmosphere, have your next rummage sale at a flea market. In addition to providing experience, it will probably be cheaper and more successful than running a newspaper ad.

Resources

- *Flea Market America: The Complete Guide to Flea Enterprise* by Cree McCree (Ocean Tree Books, 2003).
- www.keysfleamarket.com: A directory of flea markets across the United States.
- http://dollardays.com: Dollar store items as cheap as 6 cents.

CHAPTER 81

PROFITING FROM THE END TIMES

SURVIVAL SUPPLIES AND MORE SELLER

More than ever people are preparing to survive everything from the end of civilization to simple natural disasters. You can serve this growing market in a number of ways and make a good profit. You can sell survival supplies like knives and nitrogen-packed wheat. You can arrange survival seminars. You can create web sites or blogs to provide information and then monetize these with pay-per-click advertising or affiliate product referrals.

For example, I have a survival section on one of my backpacking web sites, with information on edible wild plants, making weapons in the wilderness, and more. Affiliate commissions and advertising revenue add up to only about $300 monthly, but I haven't worked on that section of the web site in years, making this a nice residual income. A more actively updated web site or blog could make thousands of dollars per month. I'm sure some of them do. A survival supply web site can be far more profitable than that. Selling emergency-preparedness manuals and e-books is another niche to consider.

Money

Tapping into this market niche by providing information means you won't have a garage full of inventory nor need to be home to process orders. On the other hand, in my experience many informational web sites average just 5 cents per visitor, so you'll need to build traffic up to about 3,000 visitors daily to net $50,000 annually. To boost that you might sell e-books and paper books, or provide free and paid newsletters.

A seven-day four-person home survival kit typically sells for $250, so it's easy to see that revenue per customer can be high in a supply business. Orders of over $1,000 are common for companies that supply specially preserved food caches along with all the usual survival weapons and tools. A retail location along with an online store might provide the most potential, although the overhead of a physical store makes this riskier. The database I checked showed only a few dozen survival supply businesses, compared with 1,600 scrap metal dealers and 2,900 chimney sweeps, so competition doesn't appear to be too stiff yet. Some of these survival supply companies are making more than $1 million annually.·

How to Get Started

An informational web site or blog is the cheapest way into the survival market. In fact, if you already have Internet access, your start-up costs can be less than $100, and overhead less than $20 monthly. Once you have some good tips and articles, you can monetize the site in several ways. You can link to affiliate products so when your visitors click through and buy something you get a commission. You can also sell advertising or place pay-per-click ads on each page. For this to pay big, you have to learn how to promote your site and generate traffic.

To sell survival supplies, you can have a fully stocked web store or you can first experiment with sales of specific items on eBay and other auction sites. This latter method allows you to get familiar with the market with a smaller investment in inventory.

Resources

- *How to Survive the End of the World as We Know It: Tactics, Techniques, and Technologies for Uncertain Times* by James Wesley Rawles (Plume, 2009): Not a business guide but a great primer on your market.
- www.2012supplies.com: Example of a survival supply business.
- http://offgridsurvival.com: A survival web site monetized with pay-per-click advertising.
- www.the-ultralight-site.com/wilderness-survival-guide.html: My own profitable survival section of my backpacking web site.
- www.dollardays.com/wholesale-survival-gear.html: Wholesale survival supplies.

PART ELEVEN

CLEANING JOBS AND BUSINESSES

I don't necessarily like cleaning, but it has always come naturally to me. I recall straightening messy shelves in grocery stores at the age of six while shopping with my mother (yes, I was an odd child). Shortly after that I discovered that my (four) brothers would pay me to do the cleaning they were supposed to do. My first "real" job was washing dishes, and I later worked for a janitorial service and also as a carpet cleaner. You may not be thrilled with cleaning for a living, but cleaning jobs and businesses happen to be some of the easiest to get into and, if you do it right, the business side can be very profitable.

Of all the ways to make money in this book, some of the more ordinary ones are in the selections that follow. However, I try to point out some different and potentially more profitable possibilities. Housecleaning is a common business, for example, but the foreclosure cleaning niche has real potential at the moment. Power-washing services are not new either, but specializing in the cleaning of garbage trucks can mean bigger profit margins. And you might not have known that almost anyone willing to clean up and tear down rides can make cash after the last night of carnivals.

CHRIS GILLMAN, CARPET CLEANER

In service industries most people work as an employee before trying to start their own business. Chris Gillman, on the other hand, saw the opportunity in carpet cleaning and jumped right in. He owned his business for 10 years before selling it—and I especially wanted to ask him about the cashing out part.

Why carpet cleaning?

I had created a maid and janitorial company and sold my share to my business partner, who did not want the payment for the carpet-cleaning machine I had purchased on the advice of one of our employees. So here I was with a carpet-cleaning machine and no experience cleaning carpet. I hit the books, took some classes, and off I went with a "fake it until you make it" attitude. I worked slowly and methodically and lo and behold was getting heralded as the best cleaner my customers had ever had.

It's unusual to start with no experience, so if a person wants to work first as a carpet-cleaning technician, how much could he or she expect to make?

The average cleaning technician gets $10 to $13 per hour or is paid on commission, at 10 to 14 percent to start.

I understand you obtained training and certification for your business and for your employees. How does that work, and is it a legal requirement?

I was a fully IICRC certified (Institute of Inspection, Cleaning and Restoration Certification) Master Cleaner and Master Restoration Technician. . . . I attended several schools and seminars. Generally they lasted two to four days each, and I ended up with 17 certifications. There is no legal requirement to obtain any certification, although the IICRC is a standard in the industry and carries a lot of weight with insurance companies and the carpet mills.

How did you get most of your new clients?

At first you need to beat the streets, tell people what you do, go door to door. . . . Well-directed advertising is beneficial. Then the most important thing of all in a service business: word-of-mouth referrals!!! And then continue to remind your established base of customers.

How much did you do in sales in your best year?

As a single truck operation, I did $235,000 my best year. (Be the best in your field, price for it, and you will make money!)

You operated in a small town. What could this business make in a larger city?

The sky is the limit. I had a friend in Saginaw, Michigan, who made $450,000 a year with two trucks and had an operational cost of about 35 percent.

I understand that there are other services you offered. What are some special niches a carpet cleaner can get into as a primary business or a good sideline?

Water damage is fantastic for fattening up your bottom line. . . . Items like ozone machines you can rent for mold-control air-purifying or general deodorization make great side revenue builders. . . . Carpet protection has a 100 to 200 percent markup . . . power vacuuming . . . many, many more.

What would you say is the minimum needed to start a carpet-cleaning business?

Depending on your credit, you can lease everything you need. . . . Out of pocket you may need a computer and printer, a phone line, and miscellaneous office supplies—around $1,000. Now, I started with a truck-mount machine and was very satisfied. . . . They are much easier to work with and do a far better job in much less time, but expect to pay about $600 to $1,000 a month to buy one.

I understand that you sold your business recently. How much did you get for it?

$180,000. . . . A good idea is to keep fantastic records including all customer contact information and try to get service contracts with larger commercial clientele if you can. This will significantly boost your ability to sell your business in time.

What other advice can you offer people who might want to get into this business as an owner or as a cleaning technician?

There is a magical secret to make more than your competitors—do your job! Many in this industry are out to screw or mislead the public. . . . Say what you are going to do, then strive to do exactly what you say.

CHAPTER 82

SUCKING UP DIRT

SPECIALTY CARPET CARE

I used to be a carpet cleaner, so I know it's hard work. On the other hand, it's also satisfying to have such well-defined tasks. You arrive at an office building or home knowing what needs to be done, and it is very obvious when you're finished. You see a dramatic improvement in a carpet when you steam-clean it, and so does your customer. Plus, there is a lot of money to be made, at least for the owner of the business. Industry experts recommend cleaning carpets every 12 to 18 months, while the actual average is every seven years, so big profits can be had in educating potential customers.

As an owner you can keep it simple by doing all the work yourself and create a decent income with a single-truck company. Or you can eventually step away from the wand (the basic cleaning tool of this industry) and hire employees to clean while you grow a much more profitable business. In either case you can specialize in any of several niches to avoid competition. You can be the RV carpet cleaner in your area, for example, or you might do primarily theaters, cleaning both the carpeted surfaces and all those upholstered chairs. Focus on customers with large, open spaces and you can work shorter hours for more pay. You might also specialize in difficult-to-remove stains.

Money

Carpet cleaners are included in "janitors and cleaners" in Labor Department statistics, employees who average $24,120 annually, with about 10 percent making more than $36,000. Some companies pay cleaning technicians a percentage of sales to encourage them to sell additional products and to find new high-dollar accounts. I know of one owner who paid his key employee 25 percent of each job.

Cleaning costs across the country average 30 cents per square foot, or about $300 for a house with 1,000 feet of carpet. Some cleaners charge up to 55 cents per foot, while others bid far below average for large, easy spaces. To clean 5,000 square feet of empty conference rooms might take only four hours, and at 20 cents per foot you would still gross $1,000. That's far above the $100 per machine-hour that some cleaners aim for. And the long-term profit potential? One database lists more than a hundred companies with revenues of $5 million or more annually. A single-truck operation can do more than $200,000 in annual sales and have a profit margin of over 50 percent if it is owner operated.

How to Get Started

To get the experience and technical knowledge necessary, it helps to be an employee first. Add training and certifications to a couple of months in the field as a cleaning technician and you should be ready to form your own company. Do market research to see what cleaners are charging near you, and whether they're keeping busy or not. Look for less competitive niches (perhaps mobile homes or churches) as a way to find clients more quickly.

Don't buy a portable unit to keep costs down. They do a poor job compared to a truck-mount steam-cleaning unit. Get financing and start it right. You will likely need at least $40,000 for a van and decent machine, or half of that for a good used setup.

Resources

- *Start Your Own Cleaning Business* by Jacquelyn Lynn (Entrepreneur Press, 2010).
- www.castlecarpetcare.com: An example of a successful carpet-cleaning company in Michigan.
- www.truckmountforums.com: A discussion forum for carpet cleaners.
- www.iicrc.org: Valuable training and certification, which can help you market yourself as a true professional.

CHAPTER 83

GET PAID BY THE BANKS

FORECLOSURE CLEANER

I hope that by the time you read this, home foreclosures are not hitting record numbers every month, but for those who clean up those houses for banks I suspect there will more than enough for years to come. If you decide to get into this interesting niche, you can offer two basic services. The first is one-time cleaning of foreclosed homes in preparation for sale. The second is to focus on maintenance contracts that involve not only the initial cleanup but also regular maintenance of the property until it is sold. This means mowing, raking, and watering the lawn; trimming bushes; taking care of flowers or other landscaping; and maintaining the interior spaces and systems as necessary.

Once you are well established and have experience, lenders and the real estate agents they hire to handle sales will come to you with work. This is especially true if there aren't many cleaning companies in your area that specialize in this niche. This is a relatively low-investment, low-risk business to start as well. If you already own a truck or van, you can be well equipped for a few thousand dollars.

Money

Pricing is difficult in this business because jobs vary so much. An occupied 1,300-square-foot home is typically cleaned for $100 to $300, depending on local prices and what's included. The same home, as an empty foreclosure, might be easier or much more difficult to clean depending on what the previous owners did before leaving. I just saw a bid of more than $6,000 on a 4,000-square-foot home, although $3,000 of that was for painting—something not often handled by cleaners. One recently interviewed foreclosure cleaner said he does 10 to 20 jobs weekly at between $250 and $2,500 each. If you did 15 jobs weekly at an average of $400, you would have $312,000 in gross sales, which is more than enough to pay an employee or two and still have a decent profit for yourself.

For extra income you might offer your services to managers of rental properties, which also provides a way for you to transition out of the foreclosure market if that is necessary when times are better for home owners. Most data sources don't separate out businesses that exclusively clean foreclosed homes, but statistics for cleaning companies in general show that hundreds of them pull in more than $500,000 annually, and a couple dozen do more than $5 million.

How to Get Started

Employment is a good way to get to know the market. Job requirements are minimal (as is the pay), and this is a growing industry, so you will likely find positions near you. Pay special attention to how your employer finds clients and bids the jobs. Befriend real estate agents who regularly hire or arrange the hiring of foreclosure cleaners for banks. Ask them about Department of Housing and Urban Development guidelines (HUD is one of the largest holders of foreclosed homes, and it has pricing caps for designated areas). When you start your own company, you'll need insurance, supplies, and a dependable vehicle. It also helps to obtain some cleaning certifications to better market yourself as a professional.

Resources

- http://start-a-foreclosure-cleanup-business.com: Information, links to resources, and an e-book on how to start and operate.
- www.cleaningforeclosures.com: Photos from the field and tips on making money from salvaged items ranging from televisions to boats.
- www.cleanoutforeclosures.com: How-to manual and forms on CD from a successful foreclosure property maintenance company in Ohio.
- www.foreclosurecleanupbusiness.org: Articles on foreclosure cleaning.

CHAPTER 84

THE MONEY IS IN THE DETAILS

AUTO-DETAILING NICHES

Americans love their cars almost as much as . . . well, enough to pay for them to be thoroughly cleaned once in a while. Auto detailers do not just wash and vacuum a car. They clean ashtrays, dashboards, floor mats, and mirrors. They take cotton swabs to the hard-to-reach places, apply treatments to leather seats, and remove stains from upholstery. They shine up tires, polish chrome, and even degrease engines.

If you have an eye for detail and few hundred dollars, you have what it takes to start this business. To make it more interesting, and to avoid competition, choose a small niche or two. You might be *the* high-end detailer in town, working only on the finest cars at higher rates. You can be the budget provider, beating all others on price by doing fast basic cleaning for those who aren't so finicky. You can specialize in recreational vehicles, semitrucks, or other business vehicles. You might also do boats if they are in abundance in your area, or motorcycles.

Money

According to costhelper.com, auto detailing runs between $58 and $89 for passenger cars, vans, and SUVs, with additional charges for optional services. These extras can really add up. In fact, some companies primarily use menu-style pricing. For example, one detailer offers hand washing for $30, waxing for $55 to $160, steam cleaning the engine for $145, mini-detail (interior only) for $35, leather cleaning and treatment for $85, headlight polishing for $65, and connoisseur's detailing (everything including the top of the engine) for $320. Other items sometimes charged as extras include pet hair removal, stain removal, odor removal, engine detailing, glass scratch removal, vinyl repair, and steam cleaning of carpets.

To make big money in car detailing, you'll need to make $40 or more per hour, so you'll still have good margins once you hire others to do the dirty work. Nice profits are possible at lower prices if you get contracts for many vehicles in one location, like a used-car lot. I found many million-dollar companies under "auto detailing" when searching business revenue data, but these typically also have full-scale car washes. On the other hand, examples of one-man operations doing $35,000 to $70,000 annually were easy to find, and one I ran across does $150,000. As a one-man operation it's a safe bet that most of that is profit. With enough clients to eventually hire some employees, the field obviously holds even more profit potential.

How to Get Started

Read up on techniques and clean your own car and those of friends to practice. If necessary you can start this business with $300 in basic supplies. You might give the owner of a car wash a percentage of your sales to use some space. Mobile auto detailing is another way to go, in which case you'll probably need to buy a good start-up kit for $3,000 or more. Doing the work at your own home isn't usually practical due to zoning rules and possible contamination of the area. Constant exposure is the issue; cleaning cars at owners' homes or places of business leaves only well-dispersed minor pollutants, and you can avoid environmental issues if you don't do engine cleaning.

Resources

- *Ultimate Auto Detailing Projects* by David H Jacobs Jr. (Motorbooks, 2003): For do-it-yourselfers, but it covers the cleaning process in detail.
- www.detailking.com: Supplies and start-up packages for auto detailers.
- www.ajautodetailing.com: An example of someone in this business.
- www.automotivedetailing.com: Information on auto detailing.

CHAPTER 85

CLEANING UP AFTER TRASH COLLECTORS

GARBAGE-TRUCK WASHER

Even garbage trucks need to be washed, but it can't be done with a garden hose. That mud and crud is on thick and sticky, on the inside and outside surfaces. Proper cleaning requires a pressure washer, also called a power washer. A heavy-duty one will shoot that water out at 3,500 psi (pounds per square inch), and much of the gunk it dislodges will come flying back at you as you work. An owner of a company in Massachusetts that washes fleets of garbage trucks says, "You look like a Dalmatian except smaller spots and it's muddy garbage." So why would you want this work? Cleaning of any kind *can* be satisfying work, since you see the results so clearly when you're done. But most people probably do it for the money.

And this is just one niche in the power-washing industry. Only a few companies rely primarily on garbage trucks for their revenue, and that lack of competition can be good for your new business, but a hundred other things can be cleaned with a pressure washer. You can specialize in one or more of them. They include houses, recreational vehicles, sidewalks, parking lots, boats, office buildings, display signs, statues, roofs, tractors, and much more.

Money

The rates you can charge depend on the niches you're in, competition in your area, and quality of service. The most effective washing requires machines using high pressure, high water-flow rates, cleaning solution, and heat, but if you're weak in one of these areas you can compensate with increases in the others. Aim for $85 or more per hour when bidding. Some in the industry say you can't make money with hot water systems after employee wages and other expenses unless you get at least $65 per hour.

Typical prices at the moment are about $50 for cleaning a garbage truck, $100 to $300 for houses, and 5 cents to 20 cents per square foot for parking lots and garage floors. A typical driveway/sidewalk combo runs $100 to $200, and a whole home (house, roof, gutters, drive, walkways, etc.) can run to $500. Buses can be cleaned for as little as $30 each if there are several in one place. Checking the listings in the business–data site Manta.com, I found one-person companies ranging from $46,000 to $110,000 in estimated annual revenue. Those with three or four employees were doing more than $200,000 annually, and one with seven employees had $500,000 in revenue. Netting 25 percent of sales is common in many service businesses, suggesting a profit of $125,000 for the latter.

How to Get Started

The equipment you'll need depends on what markets you intend to target. For light jobs like mobile homes or recreational vehicles, you can get by with a machine that produces only 1,400 psi, which can be bought for about $1,000. Expect to spend a few thousand dollars or more for a hot water machine that produces 3,000 or 4,000 psi, which is what you'll want for cleaning garbage trucks or heavy machinery. Check the regulations in your state to see if some things (like heavy equipment) need to be cleaned in special locations to prevent environmental pollution.

Resources

- www.pressurenet.net: Advice, articles, and a discussion forum for pressure washers.
- www.hydroteksystems.com/applications/hundredthings.htm: A list of 111 things that can be cleaned with a pressure washer.
- http://deserteaglepowerwash.com: An example of someone in the business.
- www.ultimatewasher.com: Pressure washers and related supplies.

CHAPTER 86

CLEANING UP AFTER CARNIES

EVENT CLEANUP WORKER

Just out of high school, my friends used to make money tearing down carnival rides and packing them up at county fairs and other events. The carnival operator would typically hire anyone who showed up at closing time on the last night (usually Sunday) and if they stayed until the job was done the next morning, they were each paid $100 cash. Events in general, whether state fairs, wedding receptions, outdoor concerts, or anything else that involves many people, leave a big mess. Cleanup help is often needed.

Beyond the opportunity to make some extra cash fast, you can establish a good business niche here, and some companies are starting to specialize in this sort of work. They come in after the fun and tear down banners, sort and recycle or throw away trash, put away chairs and tables, pack up equipment, pick up garbage, and sweep and clean. One primary service is pressure washing the paved areas where outdoor events took place. Look at the sidewalks and parking lots where carnivals or street fairs have taken place, and you'll see why this is necessary. It is often required by the property owner.

Money

As with many service businesses where clients want to know the cost beforehand, pricing can be tricky for event cleanup jobs. In general you want to charge $30 per hour for each worker needed. Since customers prefer a set bid, this means you need to learn to estimate the time and resources necessary with some accuracy so you don't lose money on a job. What to include in the work is up to you. Some services offer setup help prior to events and cleaning during them as well. For outdoor events you'll need a pressure washer to clean sidewalks, pavement, picnic tables, and possibly buildings or equipment. Given the amounts of cash handed out by carnival operators to anyone who shows up for teardown work, you might do well providing a team of workers, which saves them the trouble of looking for help.

Event cleaners are not separated out for statistical purposes, but under the category "cleaning services" at a business-research site, I found well over 1,000 companies that did more than $2 million in annual sales. It seems unlikely that you can make that kind of revenue cleaning up after carnivals and other events, but sometimes a niche is just an easier way to grow your business into the more general industry.

How to Get Started

Working for a company that specializes in event cleanup can be a good way to get to know the market. When starting your own business, you might stick to one-person jobs like wedding reception and party cleanup, to gain experience and build your business before hiring employees and taking on the big jobs. For smaller indoor jobs the brooms, mops, buckets, and basic cleaning supplies will cost only a few hundred dollars. Insurance, advertising, and a good pressure washer for outdoor jobs are some of the larger expenses you'll have when you're ready to grow your business.

Resources

- *How to Open and Operate a Financially Successful Cleaning Service: With Companion CD-ROM* by Beth Morrow (Atlantic Publishing Company, 2008): Guide for general cleaning companies, but the same principles apply.
- www.pressurewashingsystems.com/services/festival-clean-up: An example of a company that offers carnival and festival cleanup services.
- www.ultimatewasher.com: Pressure washers for cleaning rides, trailers, and paved surfaces.
- www.acceleratedwaste.com/special_event_cleanup.html: An event-cleaning specialist in the southeastern United States.

PART TWELVE

STILL MORE UNUSUAL WAYS TO MAKE MONEY

I used to play chess for money. I wasn't a real shark, meaning I never lost on purpose just to sucker someone into betting more on the next game. I just bet a few dollars when I knew my opponent was a weaker player. But playing chess is not one of the ways to make money you'll find in this section, although if you love the game like I do—and are better than me—it might be worth trying. You also won't find information on some of the other ways I've paid the bills, like packaging infomercial products, unloading trucks, hanging drywall, or selling call options on my stocks. After all, if any of those were easy enough ways to make a lot of money, I might still be doing them.

What you *will* find here is all the entries that did not fit into one of the other categories. This is the catchall part of the book, and because of that it has some of the more interesting jobs and businesses. Here you'll learn how to be a human guinea pig, sell fried butter, rent mannequins, spy on people for a living, and more.

JASON GILLMAN, SURVEILLANCE EQUIPMENT SALES

Jason Gillman has been in the surveillance industry for more than a decade. He became a surveillance technician at a small casino in Michigan where he first worked as a blackjack dealer, then started Industrial Covert Unlimited to sell surveillance equipment. His story provides a great example of how to use a job to get into a business and of the potential of home-based ventures. Gillman has moved out of his house into a new facility and now has five employees.

How did you get your first job working in the industry, and what qualifications did you need?

I talked my way into the industry, relying on my mechanical training as a marine engineer. I was able to convince the interviewers for a casino's surveillance tech position that I could handle the job they had available. I then immersed myself in all that was knowable on the subject and was up to speed very quickly.

How long did you work as an employee before starting your business?

After a couple of years designing, installing, and arranging the cameras in the casino environment, I had also developed a decent relationship with the vendors who sold to the casino. I at first approached them about buying so as to sell in a profit venture for the casino—to other casinos (relying on my expertise and familiarity with what they needed). As my employers seemed to have no interest, I pursued it then for my own future endeavors. After arranging a couple of sizable sales in my free time, I realized a full-time effort would be far more rewarding.

What do you sell the most of, and how big are some of your orders?

Average orders are between $1,200 and $2,000. I have had orders as large as $78,000 and as little as $3.

You worked out of your home for a while before moving into a larger facility. How well did that work out?

With a basement and garage full of inventory, and a single-person operation, it works great. At some point the sheer volume of business requires that it be moved, if only to maintain some form of sanity.

You carry a lot of inventory, which suggests it might be difficult to start a business like yours with a small investment. But if a person wanted to get into the surveillance industry with a consulting and installation business, could that be done for a few thousand dollars?

A credit card with a decent limit ($4,000 to $5,000) would be enough for a person with a little training and a bit more motivation. In fact, short of a massive investment in labor-saving devices, an installer could literally start with about $400 to $500 worth of equipment and be fairly efficient.

I understand that your profit margins vary according to collections and other factors, but can you tell us how much you have done in sales in your best year so far?

My best year was $1.6 million.

You must talk to a lot of installers. Do you know if some of them make more than $75,000 annually from their work?

Many do, though if I had to guess, most make around $40,000 (single-man operations).

What advice can you offer to someone who wants to work or do business in the surveillance industry?

First, study before you start . . . and ask questions. Second, work with a good distributor. . . . Too many distribution houses have salespeople who have never touched the tools, worked with the cameras, or seen the results of their work on display. A newcomer to the field can learn quite a bit from a motivated distributor who is more than willing to share bits of important information while hawking his wares. Over time, that information is invaluable. . . . Third, do not sell your system to a customer as "the most incredible system ever!" Many folks will think that they should expect a CSI-grade system at that point. Even with some of the wonderful advances in the industry, we are not yet to the level of CSI type of fictional results. Finally, do not undervalue your work. Remain competitive; however, if you are installing, remember that sometimes you will have to go back and replace parts or warranty your installation in some way. Being able to provide the best service without feeling like you did not charge enough can be its own reward.

CHAPTER 87

BE A HUMAN GUINEA PIG

MEDICAL RESEARCH SUBJECT

Volunteer for medical research? Here's the description of one current opening: "The volunteers' wisdom teeth are surgically extracted. . . ." Okay, perhaps I should clarify. The "inclusion criteria" say that subjects must actually need their wisdom teeth removed. In other words, you get paid for something that normally costs you a lot of money. That's not so bad. In fact, although some research volunteer work is dangerous (drug trials have resulted in deaths), there are some safe ways to work as a human guinea pig. Experiments run by psychologists, sociologists, and anthropologists, for example, often involve nothing more than answering questions and watching videos or computer monitors.

You can make decent money if you risk more. One truck driver in Milwaukee, after making $6,500 for taking a drug and submitting to blood tests and echocardiograms over 48 days, went on to make $80,000 volunteering for various studies. And a lot of work is available for research volunteers. It is estimated that scientists in the United States need 10 million test subjects annually.

Money

Some studies impose more discomfort than real risk and still have reasonable pay. A recent article profiled test subjects who had to have tubes in their throats for weeks to test a medical device. Uncomfortable, but they were paid thousands of dollars. A study of the Paleolithic diet paid $200 and free food for three weeks for subjects. All they had to do was eat what was given to them. Basic psychological and sociological research that involves questionnaires and simple experiments (usually in a university setting) is the safest work, and often takes less than an hour, but it can pay as little as $10 or $20.

To make the most money and to find more jobs as a test subject, you need to participate in invasive and potentially risky studies. These may involve sleep deprivation, brain imaging, vaccines, and more. Clinical drug trials offer the most consistent work. You are normally paid between $100 and $300 daily for these if you have to remain in a hospital, or $25 to $100 if they only require you to check in daily for tests. One recent study required participants to take two FDA-approved drugs already on the market to see how they interact. It involved a few blood draws but left volunteers free to eat and drink what they liked and paid them $3,300 for 23 days. Medical trials of various types can pay as much as $10,000 if they last longer than a few weeks.

How to Get Started

Inclusion criteria vary. Healthy volunteers are sometimes needed, while other studies need people with specific conditions. For example, a study in Texas currently needs children 6 to 16 years old with ADHD (attention deficit hyperactivity disorder) to test a new drug treatment (two visits, $230 total). If you have a specific condition, you can start there and possibly get free treatment as well as get paid. Check web sites where research trial openings are posted or discussion forums for test volunteers.

Resources

- *The Professional Guinea Pig: Big Pharma and the Risky World of Human Subjects* by Roberto Abadie (Duke University Press Books, 2010): A look at "professional guinea pigs" and the risks they take.
- www.gpgp.net: The URL stands for "Guinea Pigs Get Paid," and this site tells you how.
- www.unusualwaystomakemoney.com/z-guinea-pigs.html: Some basic information.
- www.wired.com/wired/archive/15.05/feat_drugtest.html: A good article about being a medical research volunteer.

CHAPTER 88

DEEP-FRIED BUTTER

UNIQUE FOOD CONCESSION BUSINESSES

Abel Gonzales Jr. won awards at the Texas state fair for deep-fried cookie dough, Coke, and peanut butter sandwiches over the years. He eventually quit his 14-year job as a computer analyst and now makes a living from his 24-day stint as a food concessionaire at the state fair each year. In 2008, along with his other dishes, he sold 40,000 orders of his most heart-stopping creation: deep-fried butter. Whipped, frozen, covered in dough, and then fried, this is a surprisingly popular food.

Thousands of entrepreneurs operate food carts or trucks at carnivals, fairs, parks, craft shows, and events of every sort, but you can avoid the competition to some extent if you specialize in something unique. You can even do what Gonzales does and use your home kitchen as your research center. Dream up a new fruit drink, create an excellent vegetarian hot dog, or bring high-end delicacies to the masses, and you can do thousands of dollars per day from a cart, trailer, or truck setup. This is a business you can do part-time if you like, perhaps working only weekends when you first start. And with no fixed overhead, you can effectively put the business away and take it out again when desired, whether because you want seasonal work or just some time off.

Money

Profits from a food concession business depend on your products, the nature of the events you work, the weather, where at the event you are located, and other factors. Low-priced items like soda can be simpler to deal with, but you need many more sales to make money. The rent for a good location can be up to hundreds of dollars daily, so you need to sell a certain amount just to break even. Even with a $4 item that costs you $1 to make, your first 100 sales can go just to covering the location fee. If you're planning to sell a particular item for a long time to come, you may want to test prices, even though this could mean making less money for a few days. You might learn, for example, that your net profit is much higher when selling 350 fish-on-a-sticks daily at $5 each than with the 400 sales you get when the price is $4.

According to the estimates at Manta.com, a few dozen food concession businesses make more than $1 million in annual sales. That level of business requires employees and more than one food cart, but with profit margins typically higher than the 25 percent that fixed-location restaurants make, some of these owners probably take home as much as $300,000.

How to Get Started

You can start a food concession very inexpensively if that's necessary. It can be as simple as buying a cooler with wheels and selling cans of juice or pop at local street fairs. That may even be a good way to see if you like dealing with the public as a food or drink vendor. But it is not something that will make you a livable income. For that you'll have to decide on the general type of business you want and buy some potentially expensive equipment, ranging from a hot dog cart to a rolling snack stand to a truck with a kitchen.

Resources

- *Food Booth: The Entrepreneur's Complete Guide to the Food Concession Business,* Second edition, by Barb Fitzgerald (Carnival Press, 2011).
- www.cmssystem.com: Food vending carts, trailers, and trucks.
- http://cruzincooler.com: A vending cooler you can ride around on.

CHAPTER 89

SECRETLY WATCHING PEOPLE

SURVEILLANCE WORKER

I worked in a casino many years ago, and although we dealers knew there were people watching everything from cameras above, we never saw them. That's the nature of working in surveillance. The employees "upstairs" were told to keep to themselves even when off-duty, and to keep watching both customers and employees. This is because, in a casino environment especially, the risk always exists of employees colluding with outside criminals, and it is important that nobody other than the surveillance team knows when they're watching, where the cameras are pointed, where the "blind spots" are, and so on.

If you like the idea of secretly watching people, this might be a job for you. But be sure you can tolerate sitting still and watching video monitors for hours on end. If not, and if you're more mechanically inclined, you could consider becoming a technician, setting up CCTV (closed-circuit television) and other equipment. Once you have enough experience, you can even start a business as a consultant and/or an installer, or you can sell surveillance products to installers.

Money

You can make a decent living as a surveillance officer (watching the monitors) or as a surveillance technician (maintaining the cameras). Labor Department statistics show the average annual income of gaming surveillance officers as $32,500 annually, with about 25 percent making more than $39,000. Working in government offices or the office buildings of some large corporations can also pay well. Wages for positions in shopping malls and department stores are usually lower.

Of course, the big money is in starting your own business. You can provide security and surveillance services, consultations, or equipment installation. Or you might sell products retail or wholesale them to installers. For an idea of what's possible in the latter area, see the interview with Jason Gillman. Dozens of surveillance equipment companies in the United States do more than $5 million in annual revenue.

How to Get Started

Currently, the biggest employers of surveillance officers and technicians are casinos, but these positions can also be found in department stores, shopping malls, and office buildings. A recent check of Craigslist.com showed offerings in virtually every major city in the country. At the moment there are even some positions advertised on cruise ships. Before you directly approach potential employers, study the industry and read about the latest equipment. Many employers want applicants to have six months' experience or more. Work as a security guard can count toward that, as can employment with a security systems installation company, and these are usually easier jobs to get. If you are hired for that position by a company that also has a separate surveillance department, you have the possibility of a promotion.

Surveillance is a tough field to get into as a business owner without previous knowledge. It is best to work as an employee in the industry first. It may also help to invest a few hundred dollars into a simple surveillance system that you can tinker with at home (perhaps setting it up to watch the babysitter).

Resources

- *Intelligent Network Video: Understanding Modern Video Surveillance Systems* by Fredrik Nilsson (CRC Press, 2008).
- http://casinocareers.com: Job listings here commonly include surveillance positions for which the only educational requirement is a high school diploma.
- www.cu1.com: Industrial Covert Unlimited sells surveillance equipment and provides wholesale CCTV pricing for resellers.
- http://en.wikipedia.org/wiki/Surveillance_cameras: An article on closed-circuit television (CCTV), covering basic equipment, how it's used, and privacy issues.

CHAPTER 90

THE PARTS ARE GREATER THAN THE WHOLE

JUNKYARD BUSINESS

As a young man I paid a junkyard $21 for a half-ounce metal piece needed to repair my blinker switch—and I had to remove it from the auto. Later I needed a headlight assembly and a door and was told the used car door would be $250 and the headlamp $50. I previously sold at least one old car to a junkyard for $35 and had bought working autos for less than $300 several times. I was starting to realize the profit potential in the things people throw away.

Also called scrap yards and salvage yards, a junkyard can take just cars, target another niche like boats or farm equipment, or accept all junk items that have salvage value. You make money by buying cheap, breaking apart what you buy, and selling the parts. Scrap metals alone can be worth more than what you pay for a junk car, and people will pay you to take old washing machines and other appliances. If you like the idea of someone *paying you* to take an old air conditioner, and then selling the scrap copper in it for $30, you might like this business.

Money

You can create a niche business based on whatever experience you have. If you know boats you might start a marine salvage yard, for example. If you already sell used appliances, you might start a small salvage operation out back, charging a fee for drop-offs and then tearing them apart for parts and valuable scrap metals. Those are the two basic ways you make money with any junkyard, by the way—sell the parts and/or sell the recyclable materials. A car might have thousands of dollars in parts, aluminum wheels worth $40, copper in the radiator worth $60, platinum in the catalytic converter worth $150, and other

221

metals. See Chapter 42 on scrap metal recycling to get an idea of the valuables you can recycle from autos and appliances.

Profit margins can be great, but you may have most of those profits tied up in inventory at any given time. The key to staying out of trouble is to find the balance between sales and the rate at which you invest in new inventory. To get an idea of the income potential from these businesses, I had to search the data under the categories of "salvage yards," "junkyards," and "scrap yards." Those searches yielded dozens of companies that do more than $2 million in annual sales.

How to Get Started

Zoning rules can be a factor as can regulations related to hazardous materials like oil, radiator fluid, batteries, refrigerants, power-steering fluid, and gasoline. A potentially large investment in inventory is required. For these reasons, it's not easy to start without experience. Working in a junkyard is one way to learn the ropes. If you live away from others, you might run a small salvage operation from home, handling only items that don't contain hazardous materials. You could pick up old appliances and strip them for salable parts and scrap metal, for example, and parlay your profits into a larger venture when you're ready.

Resources

- *Automotive Salvage Junk Yard Service Start Up Business Plan* by www .bplansnow.com (2010): An Amazon Kindle e-book; you can download a Kindle reader for your computer from Amazon.com.
- www.a-r-a.org: The Automotive Recyclers Association provides news, regulatory information, and compliance guidance.
- http://westernscrap.com: An example of a successful scrap yard.
- www.junk-yards.net: List your business in this directory of junkyards.

CHAPTER 91

YOU'VE GOT THEIR NUMBER

HOUSE-NUMBER CURB-PAINTER

A few months ago a young woman dropped off a flier offering to paint our house number on the curb for $10. It's generally a good idea to do so to make it easy for ambulance drivers and police to locate one's home, so we agreed. The following week we got a nice black rectangle on the curb, with our address painted on it in white reflective numbers. She was clearly undercharging for the quality of service, but when we later walked around the neighborhood we saw many other jobs she had done, so after the minimal expense of paint perhaps she made $100 for the day.

This is a simple business to start and operate. With less than $100 in supplies, you're ready to go. If you have a computer, you can print up fliers for pennies apiece or you can just go door to door to offer your service and do the job on the spot. You can do this as a one-person operation or expand to include employees. You can start and stop the business to fit your schedule as well. Keep in mind that you will be selling your service face to face, and although it is not a major purchase, many people will say no, so you need to become comfortable making the pitch to homeowners.

Money

Shortly after having our own curb painted, I talked to a friend who used to run his own business doing this. He hired college students and other young people to paint, and he charged $20 per job, which is necessary if you plan to have employees. He says that even using highly reflective glass-bead paint for the numbers, the materials cost only about a dollar per site, and the painting takes about 10 minutes. The bigger part of your time will be spent talking to homeowners and driving to locations. The typical price range is $15 to $20 for one-person operations.

If you paint house numbers on a dozen customers' curbs in a six-hour day, spend $12 for materials and another $6 for auto expenses, fliers, and that day's prorated liability insurance, your net profit would be $222. That's assuming you charge $20 and do the work yourself. Of course income is limited if you're the only worker. If you spend your time finding 36 customers daily and have a couple of young people do the painting for $5 commission per job, your profit will be closer to $500. Assuming bad weather allows only 140 painting days per year, you would have an annual profit of $70,000.

How to Get Started

Call the city clerk to see if you need a permit, which typically costs $30 or $40. Liability insurance is not a legal requirement but is a good idea. Buy paint and other supplies. Brass stencils or templates last forever and can be cleaned easily, making them worth the extra cost. Take photos of your best jobs to show to prospective customers. Identify good areas to prospect in, which include neighborhoods that are middle class or higher and don't yet have many curbs numbered (or have many faded numbers). Leave fliers with your phone number when nobody is home. The jobs these produce can be done all on one day for efficiency.

Resources

- *Curb Painting—Money Making Secrets Revealed!,* Fifth edition, by Jason Farber (Lulu.com, 2006).
- www.expressyouraddress.com: A company that sells curb-painting supplies to do-it-yourselfers, which is another way to make money in this industry.
- www.curbpainting.biz: This site sells a guide to curb-painting.

CHAPTER 92

PLAYING WITH PLASTIC PEOPLE

MANNEQUIN BUSINESS

Y ou can understand the sales side of this business, but did you know that people rent mannequins? They do so for parties and other events where a certain atmosphere is desired, and for events where clothing or jewelry needs to be displayed. Clothing stores sometimes rent rather than buy in order to keep their initial investment down and as a way to have regularly changing displays. Moviemakers rent them as well.

They come in various styles, ranging from simple dress frames to realistic and anatomically correct mannequins. Some in the business also sell display fixtures. Others sell the parts—people use loose arms and legs for Halloween displays or in film scenes. One company even rents out its warehouse full of mannequins to anyone who wants to use it for movies or photo and art projects. A quick Google search yields companies that both sell and rent mannequins in San Francisco; New York; Seattle; Las Vegas; Los Angeles; and Powder Springs, Georgia, among other cities. You might be the first to do so in your own town.

Money

The realistic mannequins typically retail for $200 to $400 and can be bought wholesale for as little as $100. The obvious market for sales is any and all clothing stores. If you rent mannequins, you can typically charge $30 to $50 daily, $120 to $150 weekly, and $200 or more per month. Given the reasonable cost to buy them, the profit potential in renting your mannequins is clear. To maximize revenue you'll want to sell them, rent them, and also set them up for big events. Offering repair services is another profit booster. The charge for complete reconditioning is around $120 to $140. For a store owner this represents a substantial savings versus buying a new one, so there is usually demand for repairs and reconditioning.

What's the long-term potential of this business? An article on the web site smallbusinessprof.com says that Mannequin Madness, in California, with sales of more than 2,000 mannequins annually, is expanding and moving its headquarters to Atlanta. Manta.com, a business profile site, estimates more than $500,000 in annual sales for Mannequin Recovery in Arizona.

How to Get Started

In theory, you could buy a mannequin, rent it out to recover the cost within a few weeks, and then buy another and start expanding. This bootstrapping strategy might work if no other mannequin-rental businesses are operating in your area. But realistically you'll probably want a retail location and a dozen mannequins or more, so plan on investing $10,000 or more to start.

Do some market research to be sure there is enough demand in your area. The ideal locale is a city that has grown large enough to support a business of this type but doesn't yet have one. It's good for profits when your customers have no place else to go. Sales can be made anywhere if done online, but mannequin rental is usually local. If you happen to have a mannequin business near you, you can also look for employment there as a way to learn the business.

Resources

- www.mannequinmadness.com: This company sells and rents. Its web site will give you a good idea of what's available, and the cost.
- www.displayimporter.com: Wholesale mannequins for as little as $99; shipping runs $20 and up, and you can buy one mannequin at a time.
- www.importers.com: If you are interested in importing mannequins, search the keyword "mannequins" to find Chinese manufacturers.

CHAPTER 93

A SWEET JOB

CHOCOLATIER

A confession: Along with our coffee or tea, my wife and I have been eating chocolate for breakfast for years. It's now a finer, 60 percent cacao type because tastes progress with income, so we were thrilled to see that the newest café/coffee shop that opened in our little town has its own chocolatier. A special counter and display sit at the back of the place, with all the latest carefully crafted chocolate confections. They're delicious, but they can be healthy too. Dark chocolate has an abundance of flavonols, which protect the body from aging and lower blood pressure by stimulating production of nitric oxide, and phenylethylamine and serotonin, which are both mood elevators found naturally in our brains. Regular consumption even reduces LDL cholesterol by up to 10 percent.

If you like to create delicious things to eat and have a particular fondness for chocolate, you might just have a new career or profitable business opportunity. If our little mountain town can have its own chocolatier, there is certainly room for one or two more in many other cities. And if you like, you can start your education and training in your own kitchen.

Money

Perhaps with all products, prices are partly a matter of perception, but this is especially true with gourmet chocolate. In general, prices start at $20 per pound, although fudge tends to sell for less. *Forbes* magazine recently reported on a chocolatier whose prices start at $75 per pound. It also noted that in general the $15 billion chocolate industry in the United States is moving away from sugary mass-produced products toward more expensive premium dark chocolates. Knipschildt Chocolatier, located in Connecticut, currently sells its La Madeline au Truffe, a 1.9-ounce confection, for $250. That's $2,100 per pound.

As with almost every profession, the big money is not in working as an employee, although that's a great way to start. You might even make a decent income if you work for companies catering to customers with the most refined tastes (or the most expensive tastes). Once you start your own business, you can sell online, from a store, or wholesale to other stores and coffee shops. Out of the several hundred chocolatiers listed in one business database, more than a dozen do $2 million in annual sales. These companies have typically expanded into general candy and confections, with chocolate as their primary, but not exclusive, product. One such outfit in Indiana does more than $20 million annually.

How to Get Started

You can learn the art of making chocolate confections from schools. One of the more famous ones has a branch in Chicago. Prior to that, or in place of it, you can study and practice at home for as long as it takes to build your skills and confidence. An apprenticeship under a master chocolatier is perhaps the best option, since you can make an hourly wage while you learn the craft. As you train and practice, you should consider the niche you want to work in, meaning both the types of confections you'll specialize in and the type of business. You might wholesale, retail online, open your own chocolate shop, or do all of these.

Resources

- *Making Artisan Chocolates* by Andrew Garrison Shotts (Quarry Books, 2007).
- http://en.wikipedia.org/wiki/Chocolatier: An article about making chocolate.
- www.chocolate-academy.com: The Chocolate Academy has schools around the world, including one in Chicago.
- www.the-chocolatier.com: An example of a chocolatier in New Hampshire.
- www.knipschildt.com: A high-end chocolatier.

CHAPTER 94

PUTTING IT ALL ON THE TABLE

TABLETOP ADVERTISER

Y ou may have seen, in restaurants and cafes, tables with advertising embedded in them. They sometimes also have facts about the area or photos of nearby attractions. It gives you something to look at and read while you wait for your food, or wait for the check. The ads and other items are under an acrylic coating, which makes them permanent and makes the table easy to clean. How did the tables get there? They were given to the restaurant, perhaps saving the owner a couple of thousand dollars versus buying his own.

Who gives away free tables? Companies that make their money from the advertisers. The restaurant owner typically commits to using the tables for two years. Local businesses pay hundreds or thousands of dollars to advertise where thousands of people sit each week. Your job, if you want it, is to find restaurant, bar, and café owners who want free tables (perhaps the easy part), find 20 to 40 advertisers, then have the tables made and put them in place.

Money

A typical charge is $500 for a two-year placement of an ad, per restaurant. Some charge much more. One entrepreneur I talked to prices according to the town. His two-year charge is often based on the cost to run a similar-size ad for five to six days in a local newspaper. He also says that if there are more than 20 tables in a restaurant he'll sell ads for all tables or for sets of them. Other pricing criteria include ad size, length of time (usually two years, but other payment periods are possible), and position (corners cost more). Rates compare very favorably with other options. For example, even a small-town yellow-pages ad can run thousands of dollars per year, while a $600 ad on 20 tables in a restaurant might be seen by 120,000 people in two years, for a cost per impression of a half-cent (that's your sales pitch, by the way).

Restaurant chains provide big profit potential. A California company has its tables in 54 restaurants belonging to one chain. Mall food courts are another niche to look into. How much can you make? I found several examples of companies making more than $100,000 in sales with one employee. Sell 30 spots for an average of $600 and you collect $18,000 per restaurant. Your expenses include tables, but a net of $10,000 per restaurant, with one deal per month gives you a profit of $120,000 annually. Sign up a chain of 54 restaurants and . . . well you can do the math.

How to Get Started

Many of these companies are looking for dealers or representatives, who are typically paid a percentage of sales. One of them claims on its web site that you can make "$40,000 to $75,000 working part-time from home." True or not, it's a great way to learn the business and to see if you like it and can handle the necessary sales work. In fact, the selling part (to restaurants *and* advertisers) is crucial, so if it goes well, you should be very confident about starting your own tabletop advertising business. If you're more of the managerial type than a salesman, you might partner with someone who's a good salesperson.

Resources

- www.tabletopbillboards.com: A company looking for dealers and offering 50 percent commission on advertising sold.
- www.markitbright.com: A company that makes tables for this industry.
- http://tableads.com: An example of someone in this business.
- http://activetable.com: Another example of someone in this business.

CHAPTER 95

SMALL CRACKS EQUAL BIG PROFITS

MOBILE WINDSHIELD REPAIRER

We had two rock chips in our windshield last year (Colorado is known for this problem—lots of rocks). The second one happened an hour from home, and the crack kept getting longer as I drove. I later had to replace the windshield. Next time I get a chip I'll call a mobile repair service and get it fixed before it goes too far. In fact, even if I'm at home, I like the idea of them coming to fix it while the car is in my driveway, rather than driving to the local repair shop and sitting in a waiting room. Apparently a lot of people feel the same way, since this is a growing industry.

With a mobile windshield-repair business you have a low investment initially. You can start by buying a kit for $200 to $800. You have very little overhead, assuming you find a good cell phone plan and already own a van, pickup, or other suitable car. You get to work outdoors. And you can be in business by next week if you like.

Money

For a typical chip repair you'll make $50 to $60 and use 50 cents worth of resin, so gross profit margins are good, to say the least. Of course you'll have the cost of your vehicle, a phone, liability insurance, and whatever advertising you choose to do. Radio works well for the latter, by the way, because people are listening in their cars while looking through cracked and chipped glass. Long crack repairs are priced between $90 and $150, and some repair systems claim 99 percent success for fixing cracks as long as three feet. Other services you can offer include headlight restoration (making them clear again) and minor bulb replacement for turn signals and brake lights.

How much can you make? In part it depends on pricing and the demand and competition in your local area. Chip repairs can be completed in 15 minutes, but you'll have time between jobs. Eight $50 repairs daily five days per week should net you more than $75,000 annually after every expense. Of course, with several trucks and employees you can make much more. A check of thousands of mobile windshield-repair businesses for which data is available shows many with $1 million or more in annual revenue, but a closer look at these successful companies suggests that you'll have to offer other services and possibly have a fixed location to reach this level of sales.

How to Get Started

If you're mechanically inclined, you can learn the basics of the business from books and videos. Several companies sell this kind of training online. Working for a windshield-repair company for a few weeks is another way to gain the knowledge and practice you'll need. If you prefer to pay for hands-on training, you may have to travel, but it's not expensive otherwise. Several companies that sell the repair kits and supplies offer training that lasts from one to three days, and they generally charge less than $500 if you are buying a kit from them.

Resources

- www.liquidresins.com: Windshield-repair kits from less than $300, training for less than $500, and an insurance-claim-processing service.
- www.drbobswindshieldrepair.com: An example of someone in the business.
- www.windshieldrepair.net: A web site where you can list your business.
- www.ultrabond.com: This company can show you how to fix three-foot-long cracks and save customers the cost of a new windshield.

CHAPTER 96

DRIVING OTHER PEOPLE'S CARS

CONTRACT CHAUFFEUR

I used to drive an attorney around Michigan in his car for $50 per day, which usually meant 4 to 10 hours of driving. Looking at current rates I suspect I was charging too little. But then again, he was my father, and it was 20 years ago. The basic idea is that he could bill $60 per hour working on clients' cases (imagine trying to get a lawyer that cheap now) while I drove for as little as $5 per hour.

The numbers still work today because even paying a driver $35 per hour makes sense if an attorney charges clients $250 per hour or more for work done while traveling. And that is just one market for a chauffeur. You can do pickups at nightclubs for people who need to get their car home but had too many drinks to safely do it themselves. You can drive groups from club to club all night. Executives who don't have a driver may need one so they can spend their travel time preparing for a meeting or event. Some clients just like to impress others by being chauffeured. You can do this by driving only the customer's car, or you can eventually provide a car as well. You can choose among many different niches when starting out as a contract chauffeur.

Money

In BLS statistics chauffeurs are included with taxi drivers, who average $23,930 annually. Limousine drivers often make $50,000 or more full-time, with wages and tips. If you're the owner of a chauffeur service, you'll have more freedom. You'll also make much more money if you eventually invest in vehicles and employees. Designated-driver and other chauffeuring using the client's own car typically runs $35 per hour plus a 20 percent tip, with a three-hour minimum, or $45 per hour for more formal service (suit and tie, opening doors for clients), so a five-hour night can be $270. As an owner/driver, most of that would be profit (you'll have to get to their location and it's a good idea to have liability insurance).

When you provide the car, rates start as low as $50 per hour for a decent sedan, and go as high as $150 per hour for larger limousines, usually with a three-hour minimum. If you decide to start your own company, you have good reason to offer limousine service. Of the dozens of chauffeur services that do more than $1 million in annual revenue in the United States, almost all offer limousines to clients.

How to Get Started

Most states require a chauffeur's license, which is often just an endorsement to your existing license and requires a simple written test. Working as an employee is a good way to start, and the experience will make it easier to market your own chauffeur service when you're ready. If you begin your business by driving only clients' cars, it will keep costs down and leave you able to choose when to work to some extent. After some time, you can decide if you want to expand by hiring employees and/or investing in cars or limousines.

Resources

- *Careers for People on the Move and Other Road Warriors* by Marjorie Eberts (McGraw-Hill, 2001): Covers many driving jobs and businesses.
- www.xclusivechauffeurs.com: A directory to list your services in, as well as news and information for chauffeurs.
- www.thesedancompany.com: An example of a company that offers chauffeurs who drive the client in his or her own car.
- www.limoschool.com: Offers training and certification.

CHAPTER 97

MAKING ROOM FOR
MORE STUFF

SHED-INSTALLATION BUSINESS

Years ago, when my wife and I moved to Tucson, Arizona, we looked at various businesses for sale, and one of them was a shed-installation company. This company sometimes sold the sheds as well, but their primary service was installing sheds that people bought as kits or raw lumber from Home Depot, Lowe's, and other home improvement stores. No experience necessary, the sellers promised. They would train me in a day or two. We decided against buying their company, but it was intriguing.

If you are handy with a hammer and a few basic power tools, this business is relatively easy to get into. If you start by providing installation services only, you'll need nothing more than some practice and an investment of a few hundred dollars in tools. You can expand from there to selling the sheds you install. With a few employees, and in an area with enough population, this business can become very profitable. And you get to work outdoors.

Money

The company we looked at netted only about $50,000 per year, on sales of less than $100,000, and had one or two part-time employees who helped with installation. Most sheds are sold with setup included, making it tough to say what the stores are paying installers, but at least one online vendor separates out the installation in its price list. Its installation charge is $425 for a 6-by-8-foot shed (the smallest size they do), $525 for one that is 8 by 12 feet, and more for larger ones. If you sell the sheds as well, prices vary by materials (vinyl and cedar both cost more than pine), but typical pricing for basic units is $1,400 to $1,800 for a 6-by-8-foot shed and $2,200 to $2,800 for one that is 10 by 12 feet, with installation included. Price your service and/or sales so

235

you'll make at least $40 per hour when the shed is installed, which allows you to hire employees and still make a decent profit.

To expand your business and diversify your income, you can offer other services such as doghouse delivery and assembly, deck building, and old shed removal. Consider anything else people would rather not build or assemble by themselves and you might discover a new market. If you can hit that $40-per-hour target and find enough business to fill 30 hours weekly, your annual income would be over $60,000. Netting $20 per hour from three full-time employees would mean a yearly profit of $124,000.

How to Get Started

If you happen to need one, put together a shed for yourself and take photos to start your portfolio. You should also carefully track the total time spent on the installation for future reference, although you'll get quicker with experience. Let hardware and home improvement stores know you're available. You can sometimes advertise inexpensively in the service guide part of newspaper classified ads as well. Check the local regulations regarding permits for sheds. If you're going to sell the sheds you install, choose a good supplier of kits or raw materials (if you build your own designs). With a contractor's license you should be able to get a discount at the big home improvement stores. As previously mentioned, price the jobs so you have the option of hiring help when the time comes.

Resources

- *Smart Guide: Sheds: Step-by-Step Projects* (Creative Homeowner, 2009).
- www.cwtrucking.net: An example of a company that installs sheds.
- www.saltspraysheds.com: Another shed sales and installation company.

CHAPTER 98

RUGS FOR STUDENTS

NECESSITIES RENTER TO COLLEGE STUDENTS

Years ago I read an article about a man who rented carpet to college students. That's right, he bought large area rugs and even discount carpet remnants, rented them to dorm room residents who didn't like cold floors, and at the end of their stay he rolled the pieces up, cleaned them, and rented them out again. I don't recall what he charged, but he was making a good living. He generally recouped his investment in a rug the first year and rented it for many years. It was a simple business and a great example of how you can avoid competition in small niches. In fact, since I can't currently find an example of someone doing this, it might still be a good market to get into.

Renting all sorts of items to college students makes sense. They often don't have the money to buy everything they might need and will have to get rid of things they buy when they move back to their hometowns. Dorm rooms may come with beds and some basic furniture, but students still want things like a television, a dresser, a microwave, and more. Provide these to students in dorms, apartments, fraternity and sorority houses, and you can make a decent profit.

Money

If you live in an area with enough college students, you might do well in a very specialized niche, like carpets or kitchen appliances. Otherwise it is best to carry a wide variety of items. Items are rented by the semester. An example of pricing at one company for a nice futon is $80 for one semester, $130 for two, and $170 for three. For the first semester it charges $35 for a coffee table, $40 for a television set, $50 for a mini-fridge, and $20 for a DVD player, with discounts for additional terms. If you are doing the math in your head, you've probably noticed that the cost of an item is generally recovered in a year to 18 months. Charging enough to recover the cost in three semesters is a good guide to pricing. Since most of these items will last five or six years (still only half the life they would have if rented to nonstudents), you should roughly quadruple the money you invest in inventory.

Your potential income depends on the scale you choose. Working alone, with 500 items rented out at an average of $120 per year, your gross revenue would be $60,000, which should net you about $40,000. With more clients and a few employees, you could top $100,000 annually for yourself. There must be money in renting items to students because one of Warren Buffet's companies does this.

How to Get Started

Without a major investment at some point, your income will be very limited. Even renting out 100 large area rugs for $30 per term, and getting two terms per year, requires an investment of $10,000 (at $100 per rug) to make a part-time income of $6,000 annually. The only reason to start small (but it's a good one) is to get a feel for the business and what's in demand before you mortgage the house and spend $100,000 on furniture, appliances, and other inventory.

Resources

- http://evolvingvox.com: An example of a dorm furniture and appliance rental business.
- www.dormgear.net: The dorm supplies sold here might give you ideas for new rental items.
- www.cort.com/student: Owned by Warren Buffet's Berkshire Hathaway, this furniture rental company markets to students.

CHAPTER 99

BEATING THE HOUSE

GAMBLER

When I worked at a casino, we played a fast version of poker called *hardball*, which was designed to allow many hands during the 15 minutes we spent in the break room every hour. Each player anteed and was dealt all but one card, then made a final bet to get the last card. If the game was "1-3," for example, each player bet a dollar, and after seeing his cards decided to put $3 more in the pot or fold. It was in these games that I learned the number one rule for winning consistently at poker (which I did, by the way): Play against weaker players. Beyond that, I cannot get into strategy here.

Most states in the country have poker rooms now, and you can win at casinos in other ways as well. You can learn to "count cards" playing blackjack, for example, to put the odds in your favor. Getting the odds in your favor is the only way to win in the long run. You can even win at roulette games with biased wheels. I used to run the roulette tables, and I watched one young man win $80,000 over the months. I even talked to him after I quit to discover exactly how he did it. See the resources section for more on that story. In Las Vegas, some people put the odds in their favor by using promotional offers and coupons. They may make only $100 to $200 nightly, but they can do so consistently with little risk.

Money

Gamblers and their winnings aren't tracked by government statisticians or others, so what we know about their income is anecdotal. Some regulars where I worked made money consistently, and the basic systems for doing so are simple but not easy. They require discipline and a stomach that can handle ups and downs. The bias in the wheel that my winning roulette player identified allowed him to make $60 per hour long term, but he still had nights when he lost $700 or $800. And the 1 percent edge that card-counting might give you at blackjack will make you just $8 per hour if you bet an average of $10 per hand to avoid big ups and downs. Plus, like "charting" a roulette wheel or playing perfect poker, card-counting can be very tedious. Then again, if it makes you $80,000 per year, it might be worth it.

How to Get Started

Choose a niche based on your personality. If you can handle the tedious nature of it, you might sit for hours systematically exploiting a biased roulette wheel, for example. Be ready for rude comments from superstitious players if you make the unusual bets required to beat the blackjack tables. Poker is the one casino game in which you play against other players rather than the "house" and so it offers the greatest potential for a regular income. Study well and practice in a free online poker room before you start investing your money.

Resources

- *Every Hand Revealed* by Gus Hansen (Citadel, 2008): Learn poker from a professional.
- *Get the Edge at Roulette* by Christopher Pawlicki (Bonus Books, 2003): How to find and exploit biased wheels.
- www.thebulletpoint.com/poker.html: An interview with a part-time poker player, and some tips on how to win.
- www.thebulletpoint.com/roulette.html: My own story of a man I watched win $80,000 playing roulette—and exactly how he did it.
- www.twoplustwo.com: Books, articles, and forums for those who make money from gambling.

CHAPTER 100

WHAT TO DO WITH AN IOU

NOTE-BROKER

You shouldn't plan to make thousands of dollars your first week note-brokering, as some get-rich-quick gurus suggest, but it *is* a fascinating business that has real potential. To understand how it works, imagine a retired couple sold their house to a young man who couldn't get a bank loan. He gives them a "note" (backed by a mortgage on the house) for $110,000, on which he makes monthly payments with 6 percent annual interest. Later the couple needs money, and the man still owes $100,000 but he has 13 more years to pay. Fortunately, some investors will buy such debt, but they won't pay face value. Let's say one will pay $88,000 for the $100,000 note. Now, what a broker does is find that buyer, and the owners of notes, and puts the two together. In this case, for example, you might tell the couple you can get them $84,000 for their note, and when your buyer pays $88,000, you keep the difference—the profit for your service. Notice that you don't have to invest any of your own money since you line up a buyer at the same time you find the seller. That's note-brokering.

Money

You *could* make thousands of dollars your first week, just by the chance discovery of a good note. The problem is finding enough opportunities to have a consistent income. Searching county records for seller-created mortgage loans or land contracts (also called a *contract for deed* in places) is time consuming, and cold-calling note-holders may teach you to handle rejection, but without being too profitable. To do this right, you'll eventually need to find the right advertising mediums to have customers calling you.

Fortunately it's true that you can start with a few hundred dollars, and there *are* many billions in notes whose owners would like to sell but don't know how. I met a note broker at a real estate seminar who was doing five or six deals per month and making $4,000 to $5,000 per transaction. Just one deal per week that nets $3,000 on average adds up to an annual revenue of $150,000.

How to Get Started

You need a buyer (or buyers) lined up before searching for sellers. Find one with clear guidelines about what he wants in terms of size, interest rates, aging (most want a year of on-time payments to consider buying a note), and the borrower's credit rating. The better you know your buyer's requirements, the easier it is to locate the right seller.

Advertise constantly in an inexpensive newspaper to find note holders ("Collecting payments and prefer cash now? Call us . . ."). Regularity is important because people see the ad over time and when they're ready to sell they turn to the most recent issue of the paper to find it. Typically, when you locate a note holder who might sell, you gather the necessary information, forward it to a buyer who makes an offer, and then you make a lower offer to the seller, creating the spread—which is your profit. Professional buyers will close deals for you and cut you a check for the difference, so sellers don't know how much you made.

Resources

- *Cash in on Cash Flow* by Laurence Pino (Simon & Schuster, 2005).
- www.brokeropp.com: Charter Financial trains you and is a buyer for the notes you find.
- http://papersourceonline.com: A note broker that is giving away a free course.

CHAPTER 101

ANIMAL POOP COFFEE ANYONE?

RARE AND UNUSUAL FOODS SELLER

I was 16 and hitchhiking across the country when I stopped in a small shop in San Francisco to buy dried, salted cuttlefish. I didn't know it was a type of squid nor what to do with it. I assumed it was fish jerky, ready to eat as a snack. It was bit salty to say the least (do you soak it and cook it perhaps?). I've always liked trying unusual foods, so I've eaten porcupine, rat snake, coral fungi, thistle stalks, and dozens of other uncommon dishes, which brings us to one I may not try, but which I might like to sell.

Kopi luwak is coffee retrieved from the excrement of civets, small Asian animals that eat coffee berries and partially digest the seeds. The "beans" are washed and roasted, creating a brew that is said to be less bitter than most. Yes, you read that right, and no, I'm not thrilled about drinking coffee salvaged from poop, but to sell it . . . well, it *is* the most expensive coffee in the world. And it's just one example of many rare and unusual foods you can build a business on. Some quick Internet research yields the following rare foods for which there are already customers: smoked eel, wild leeks, grasshoppers, cactus fruit, fufu (pounded African yam in peanut sauce), nettles (better than spinach—I've eaten this), Lady Godiva squash, and striped toga eggplants. And don't ignore the many as-yet-unmarketed delicacies, which can be great products if you want to avoid competition.

Money

Let's start with the excrement turned into gold, kopi lupak. At the moment it sells for around $190 per pound, or $120 for a half-pound. Then there is the $500-per-pound moose cheese made in Sweden; matsutake mushrooms at up to $1,000 per pound; and almas caviar from Iran, which you can sell for $25,000 per pound, although some vendors offer small $800 tins for those on a budget.

How much can you make with strange delicacies? It is difficult to say, but there is clearly some money in odd foods, and I suspect you'll find especially good profit margins with $1,000-per-pound mushrooms and expensive caviar. I did locate a handful of companies under the category "rare foods" when searching a business-data web site, and a few of them topped $100,000 in annual revenue.

How to Get Started

You can start by buying and selling foods that are already known as rare and expensive. If you want to do this on the Internet from home, first try items that store easily and have a long shelf life, like pine seeds, dried herbs, and perhaps pickled roots of various plants. To grow your business faster with free publicity, look for products nobody is promoting widely. In Ecuador, for example, I've eaten piticaya (a sweet cactus fruit), cherimoya (a fruit Mark Twain called "the most delicious fruit known to men"), tomate de árbol (tree tomato), and other foods that I've never seen imported to the states . . . yet. Spruce beer is home-brewed by individuals, and you can find recipes online, yet not one company appears to be distributing it, despite an abundance of the key ingredient—spruce needles. That's an opportunity.

Resources

- www.animalcoffee.com: A seller of kopi luwak, made from coffee beans collected from civet droppings.
- www.wildrecipes.com: Some unusual recipes you might use to create new products to market.
- www.cameldairy.com: A seller of camel milk.
- www.earthy.com: An example of a company that sells many rare, unique, and unusual foods.

INDEX